Folk Foods

of the Pine Barrens
of New Jersey

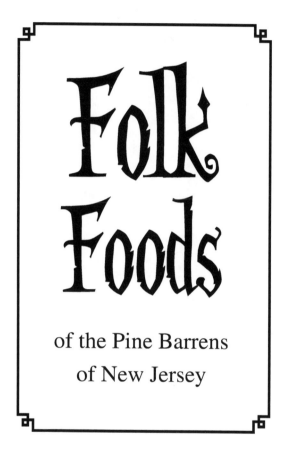

Folk Foods

of the Pine Barrens
of New Jersey

R. Marilyn Schmidt

KFR
Communications, LLC

Folk Foods of the Pine Barrens of New Jersey

First edition copyright © 2006 by R. Marilyn Schmidt
Published by Pine Barrens Press, a division of
Barnegat Light Press, Chatsworth, NJ

Second edition copyright © 2012 by R. Marilyn Schmidt
Cover art copyright © by Andrew Gioulis
Book design by KFR Communications

Published by: KFR Communications, LLC
            148 Hawkin Rd
            New Egypt, NJ 08533

Publisher's Note: The author and publisher have taken care
in preparation of this book but make no expressed or implied
warranty of any kind and assume no responsibility for errors or
omissions. No liability is assumed for incidental or consequen-
tial damages in connection with or arising out of the use of the
information contained herein.

ISBN-10: 098289595X
ISBN-13: 978-0-9828959-5-5

Printed in the United States of America

www.kfrcommunications.com

Contents

INTRODUCTION

When industry - iron mills, paper mills, glass factories - left the pines, the economy reverted again to agriculture and forging. While urban areas flourished with an industrial market, the pinelands again became a rural region even more isolated from the city.

Because of their often perceived or actual isolated location, Pine Barrens folk grew much of their food, particularly fruits and vegetables. Chickens were kept for meat and eggs; hogs supplied smoked hams, sausage, tallow, and even pig skin. Deer, rabbits, squirrels, wild turkeys, snappers, and other animals were eaten as needed. Cows, less common, supplied milk and beef. Some inhabitants kept goats and sheep. People of the pines knew how to live off the land.

During the Great Depression, these residents suffered little hardship. Gardens supplied vegetables which were eaten fresh, dried or canned in contrast to today's freezing. Root cellars, a rarity today, enabled folks to keep potatoes, cabbages, carrots, beets, squash, and other vegetables and fruits to provide food throughout the winter.

Pine Barrens folks ate well. Little food was purchased. Necessities such as sugar, molasses, salt, pepper, flour, and cornmeal were available at the local general store.

The Pine Barrens of New Jersey is noted for cranberries and blueberries, crops which supported a large part of the populace for many years. At harvest time entire families worked in the fields. Children picked blueberries and cranberries practically from the time they could walk until the days of mechanical harvesting (mid 20th century).

In the pines, neighbors shared; they cooked from scratch; unlike today when many folks run to the local supermarket to purchase something to defrost and serve for dinner. Interestingly, today many people in the pines continue the old traditions. Cakes are still baked from scratch, gardens are maintained and yes, some people still keep chickens.

In Chatsworth, it is not uncommon to have fresh eggs from free-range chickens delivered to your door, not as in the old days, but by a tall handsome gentleman driving a late model sports car. He cheerfully presents you with one or two dozen wonderful fresh eggs from the hens which have escaped the appetite of the local fox.

In times of need - death, illness, childbirth - neighbors will arrive on your doorstep with a freshly made rice pudding or cake. At Christmastime, cookies - varieties too numerous to mention - are delivered to your doorstep by a thoughtful neighbor. The traditions of yesteryear continue today and undoubtedly and hopefully will be passed on to be continued by future generations.

Recipes included here are of historical and interesting dishes including products commonly available or locally grown. They are culled from old time literature - magazines, newspapers, books - and friends both old and new. Many were handed down from generation to generation.

Recipes are frequently shared among neighbors but there are always those who only hand down recipes to family members. Unlike today, visiting among neighbors, friends, and relatives was common. If invited into a piney home, expect a warm welcome and a "dish of tea" or cup of coffee with a tasty homemade delight. Hard cider or applejack "Jersey Lightning" - a local product, was always available for special occasions.

Good cooking is a high art. American and Pinelands cookery has a proud tradition. People from many areas, countries, and cultures have contributed to it. The foods worked with were those available from home gardens, friends, and forests. Classic dishes were prepared from local produce. Relatively simple recipes are enhanced by the flavor of fresh ingredients.

In the 1820's, Americans were accustomed to the heavy unadorned farm fare of colonial days such as the foods offered in taverns and hotels of the period. Food was prepared to fill the belly on a take-it-or-leave-it basis.

By 1825, New York was the goal of thousands of people from throughout the world. Millions of strangers arrived on our shores bringing with them the dining habits of their homeland.

During the years before the American Revolution (1776), fireplaces began to be reduced in size as fuel grew scarcer. By 1850, many old fireplaces were boarded up and stoves, a cast iron box with two stove lids at the top, were used.

After 1850, wood ranges were used for cooking. They were economical in fuel consumption and relatively easy to clean. They also provided a good place to dry socks and they increased the comfort of the family cat! As the kitchen shrank in size, the dining room appeared, followed by the Victorian parlor.

Until the middle of the nineteenth century, kitchens were usually in the basement or attached behind the house. First floor kitchens and dining rooms then became popular.

In 1890, gas ranges first appeared. The first electric stoves were displayed at the World's Fair of 1893. By 1913, reliable electric stoves were on the market.

Before 1916, ice boxes were used to store food. Ice was cut from local ponds and stored in sawdust in the local ice house. In 1916, electric refrigerators were sold for $908! By

1941, refrigerators were indispensable. After WWII freezers were common. All of these developments changed the way of life of people - even in the Pines.

The local country store played a major role in each community. Not only was it the source of supplies - that is - products not grown in the home garden, the store often served as the post office and also as the place for meeting, tying together surrounding farms into a single community. By the late nineteenth century, housewives used Mason jars (developed in Crowleytown in the Pine Barrens), egg beaters, and matches!

At the country store, exchange of commodities took place. Goose feathers were exchanged for molasses; potatoes for salt; cherry boards for tropical dyes; hemlock bark for tea and coffee beans. Women purchased their needed household items, such as fabric and thread. Importantly, the store provided a place of social interaction. Men gathered to resolve public issues and tell merry tales of mighty liars and sexual misadventures.

With the coming of the railroad (mid 1800s), life changed. Products from the cities - house rakes, mowing machines, flowered wallpaper, ingrain carpets, women's fashions, ruffled curtains - became common. Life was changing in the pines.

Young girls first learned to cook from their mothers and grandmothers. One of the first cookbooks, American Cookery by Amelia Simmons (1796), lists recipes for Cranberry Sauce, Pumpkin Pie, Mince Pie, and Watermelon-rind Pickles.

After the 1820's, more cookbooks became available. Common recipes included Corn Chowder, Roast Oysters, Bouillabaisse, Turtle Soup, Fried Mexican Beans, and Gooseberry Fool.

Other dishes of the past included Blackberry Grunt, Indian Pudding, Sweet Corn caramelize in its own husks, Cranberry Sauce, Steamed Clams, Baked Cod, Baked Beans, Brown Bread, and Blueberry Slump.

In the early days, bread was unheard of. Flour was rare; if available, bread was made with eggs of wild birds, cooked in grease in a frying pan or baked before the fire.

Hardtack, pilot bread, was common. It was simply a mixture of flour and water, then baked. Because hardtack stayed edible for months, it consequently, was an item on every ship. Have you wondered what cooks used before the development of baking powder? Pearl-ash, purified potash, was used!

Sugar was a rarity and expensive. The colonists used maple syrup to sweetened foods. Sugar maple trees grow in some areas of the pinelands but harvesting sap isn't seen today. Two sugar maple trees grow along Route 563 by Buzby's Chatsworth General Store. Today, sap from sugar maple trees is collected in North Jersey - the Mendham area - and maple syrup made. Buzby's Chatsworth General Store sells this New Jersey maple syrup.

*The recipes which follow are from old friends,
old literature, and old times! Try them.*

Cranberries

Initially cranberries were harvested from the wild bogs in the fall. Old timers say that the harvested small wild cranberries were sweeter and had more cranberry flavor that our cultivated berries of today. Enjoy cranberries the way your forefathers did.

Cranberries, long served as a sauce only at Thanksgiving and occasionally Christmas, were consumed by our forefathers in far more inventive dishes than we encounter today.

CRANBERRY MUFFINS   *Makes 12 to 15*

2 cups flour, all purpose, sifted

2 teaspoons baking powder

3 tablespoons sugar, granulated

1/2 teaspoon salt

1 cup cranberries, fresh, halved if large

1/2 cup confectioners= sugar

1 egg

1 cup milk

3 tablespoons butter, melted

Heat oven to 400°F. Grease or paper line muffin tins. Set aside. Into a large bowl, sift together flour, baking powder, sugar, and salt; set aside.

In a small bowl combine cranberries with confectioners sugar; set aside.

In a large bowl, beat egg vigorously; stir in milk, then the flour combination, and butter. Stir as little as possible; batter will be lumpy. Gently fold in cranberries.

Spoon batter into muffin tins. Bake at 400°F for 20 to 25 minutes, or until a toothpick tested in center comes out clean. Transfer pan to a rack and cool. Serve warm or cold.

CRANBERRY NUT BREAD   *Makes one 5x9-inch loaf*

2-1/2 cups flour, all purpose

1 cup sugar, granulated

1-1/2 teaspoons baking powder

1 teaspoon salt

1/2 teaspoon baking soda

2 egg whites, large, lightly beaten

1 egg, large, lightly beaten

1 cup orange juice, fresh

1 cup vegetable oil

2 tablespoons orange zest, grated

2 cups cranberries, fresh (halved if large)

1/2 cup pecans (or walnuts), chopped coarse

Heat oven to 350°F. Lightly oil a 9x5-inch loaf pan; set aside.

In a mixing bowl, whisk flour, sugar, baking powder, salt, and baking soda; set aside.

In a small bowl, whisk egg whites, egg, orange juice, oil, and orange zest. Add liquid ingredients to dry ingredients, mixing just until combined. Fold in cranberries and nuts.

Transfer batter to baking pan. Bake at 350°F for 50 to 60 minutes, until a cake tester inserted in the center of the loaf comes out clean. Cool on a rack. Delicious served plain or with cream cheese or butter.

CRANBERRY SAUCE *Serves 4 to 6*

4 cups cranberries, washed, picked over

2 cups sugar, granulated

1-1/2 cups water

In a large pot, combine sugar and water. Bring to a boil and cook for 10 minutes.

Add cranberries, cover, and cook until they stop popping. Skim off froth; discard.

Cool before serving. Add a dash of cognac if you wish.

CRANBERRY WALNUT PIE   *Makes one 9-inch pie*

2 cups cranberries, washed, dried

1 cup sugar, granulated

1/4 cup water

1 cup corn syrup

2 tablespoons butter

4 eggs

2 cups walnuts, chopped coarse

1 teaspoon vanilla

1 9-inch pie shell, unbaked

Heat oven to 375°F.

In a saucepan over medium heat, cook cranberries, sugar, water, and corn syrup until cranberries pop and mixture is rather thick. Stir in butter, remove from heat, and cool.

In a bowl, beat eggs until frothy. Stir into cranberry mixture. Stir in walnuts and vanilla.

Pour mixture into unbaked pie shell. Bake at 375°F for about 40 minutes, or until filling is firm.

Serve at room temperature with whipped cream or vanilla ice cream, if desired. It's delicious plain!

CRANBERRY-APPLE CRUNCH   *Serves 4*

6 tablespoons sugar, granulated

1/4 cup water

3/4 cup cranberries, fresh, washed, dried

2 apples, medium, peeled, sliced as needed

Topping

1/2 cup oatmeal

1/4 cup flour, all purpose

1/3 cup brown sugar

3 tablespoons butter

In a small bowl combine all dry ingredients. Cut in butter until crumbly. Set aside.

Crunch

Heat oven to 350°F.

In a large saucepan combine water and sugar; boil for 2 minutes. Add cranberries and boil 2 minutes more.

Fold in apples; transfer mixture to a baking dish. Sprinkle topping over fruit mixture.

Bake at 350°F for 40 minutes. Cool and serve with whipped cream or ice cream, if desired.

CRANBERRY FOOL *Serves 4 to 6*

1 pint cream, heavy

1 cup sugar, granulated

2 cups cranberries, fresh, washed, dried

2 tablespoons confectioners sugar

1 lime, juice of

4 ounces sour cream

In a large chilled bowl, beat together cream and confectioners sugar until quite firm and peaks form.

In a food processor or blender, combine cranberries, granulated sugar, lime juice, and sour cream. Process until well blended.

Gently and thoroughly fold in whipped cream. Allow to stand 1 to 2 hours in refrigerator to set up.

Serve in champagne or cocktail glasses. Garnish with extra whipped cream if desired.

CRANBERRY-POTATO PANCAKES   *Serves 2*

1 4-oz. package cranberries, dried, sweetened

1 potato, large, grated fine

1 onion, medium, grated fine

1 egg

1 cup milk

1 cup pancake mix

In a large bowl, combine egg, and milk; mix well. Add potato and onion.

Add cranberries and pancake mix, adding a little more or less of pancake mix to reach desired batter consistency.

Spoon batter onto hot, greased griddle; cook as you would for regular pancakes. Delicious served with applesauce!

Blueberries

Blueberries - low bush or high bush, huckleberries, whortleberries, dangleberries, billiberries - all are members of the Vaccinium and Gaylussacia families. All are cooked the same. Some are sweeter than others, some are blue, some are black. All are delicious. One difference is that black huckleberries have tiny, hard seeds. In the others, the seeds are negligible and soft.

As children it was expected that you would pick berries. The end result was delicious dishes such as Blueberry Muffins or Pancakes for breakfast, Blueberry Crisp or Cake for dessert. All great treats. Money earned picking the berries provided funds for clothing and supplies for school. Many a family earned enough to clothe their families for the year.

In 1870, New Jersey became the leading producer of blueberries. The highbush blueberry was invented in 1911, in New Jersey by Elizabeth White and F. Coville.

Blueberries are grown commercially primarily in Atlantic and Burlington counties. Over 8,000 acres are planted in cultivated blueberries. The crop is worth in excess of $38 million!

Today blueberries are recognized as a health food because of their high antioxidant content. In 2003 the blueberry was designated the state fruit of New Jersey.

BLUEBERRY MUFFINS *Makes 12*

1-1/2 cups flour, all purpose

1-1/2 teaspoons baking powder

1/4 teaspoon salt

5 tablespoons butter, softened

1/2 cup sugar, granulated

1 egg

1/2 cup milk

1 cup blueberries, fresh, washed, dried

Heat oven to 400°F. Grease muffin tins or use paper liners; set aside.

In a medium bowl, sift together flour, baking powder and salt; set aside.

In a large bowl, cream butter and sugar until it is smooth and fluffy. Beat in egg vigorously.

Stir in flour combination with milk, alternating and ending with flour.

Fold in blueberries. Spoon mixture into muffin tins. Bake at 400°F for 25 to 30 minutes, until lightly browned.

Cool on a rack. Serve warm or cold.

BLUEBERRY CRISP   *Serves 6*

3 cups blueberries, fresh, washed, dried

1/2 cup sugar, granulated

1/4 teaspoon nutmeg, ground

1/4 teaspoon cinnamon, ground

1 tablespoon lemon juice

1/2 teaspoon lemon rind, grated

3/4 cup flour, all purpose

Crumb Topping

1/2 cup sugar, white or light brown

6 tablespoons butter, softened

1/4 teaspoon salt

1/4 cup walnuts (or pecans), chopped

1 cup flour, all purpose

Heat oven to 350°F.

Crisp

In a large bowl, combine blueberries, sugar, spices, lemon juice and rind; mix gently. Transfer mixture to a 1- to 2-quart baking dish.

Crumb Topping

In a small mixing bowl, combine flour, sugar, salt, and butter. With pastry blender or fingers, combine ingredients to a crumbly consistency. Sprinkle crumbs over berry mixture.

Bake in 350°F oven for 30 minutes, or until topping is nicely browned.

Serve warm with whipped cream or vanilla ice cream, if desired.

FRESH BLUEBERRY CAKE   *Serves 9*

2 eggs, separated

1/4 cup sugar, granulated

1/2 cup butter

1/4 teaspoon salt

1 teaspoon vanilla extract

3/4 cup sugar, granulated

1-1/2 cups flour, all purpose

1 teaspoon baking powder

1/3 cup milk

1-1/2 cups blueberries, fresh, washed, dried

Heat oven to 350°F. Grease and flour bottom of a 9x9-inch baking pan; set aside.

In a medium bowl, beat egg whites until stiff. Add 1/4 cup sugar, and salt; set aside.

In a large bowl, beat egg yolks with 3/4 cup sugar and butter; beat until creamy.

Coat blueberries with a little flour; set aside.

To the egg yolk mixture, add flour and baking powder alternately with milk and vanilla. Fold in egg whites, then blueberries.

Transfer mixture to prepared baking pan. Sprinkle top with sugar and a few berries. Bake at 350°F for 50 minutes, or until a toothpick comes out dry. Do not underbake.

Great served with whipped cream or ice cream.

BLUEBERRY PIE   *Serves 6*

Crust
1 cup flour, all purpose
1 tablespoon vinegar, white
4 ounces butter
1 tablespoon sugar, granulated

Filling
1 pint blueberries, fresh, washed, dried
1 teaspoon cinnamon, ground
2 tablespoons sugar, granulated
2 tablespoons butter

Heat oven to 350°F.

Crust
In a medium bowl combine all ingredients; mix until well combined. Press into a 9-inch pie pan.

Filling

Place blueberries in pie shell. Sprinkle with cinnamon, sugar, and butter.

Bake at 350°F until crust is golden brown and berries are soft.

Additional berries may be added on top of pie after it is removed from the oven. Serve warm or cold.

BLUEBERRY POT PIE   *Serves 4*

Blueberry Sauce

2 cups blueberries, fresh, washed, dried

1/2 cup sugar, granulated

1 cup water

1 tablespoon lemon juice

In a 4-quart saucepan, combine blueberries, sugar, water, and lemon juice.

Over moderate heat, cook until berries are barely tender. Remove from heat; set aside.

Dumplings

1 cup flour, all purpose

2 teaspoons baking powder

1/4 teaspoon salt

1 teaspoon sugar, granulated (optional)

1/2-3/4 cup milk

As desired - cream, whipped or heavy

In a large bowl, sift flour, baking powder, salt, and sugar together.

Stir in sufficient milk to make a dough that will drop readily from a spoon.

Return Blueberry Sauce to stove over low heat; bring to a simmer.

Drop dumpling dough by tablespoon over the blueberry sauce. Cover pan tightly and cook 15 to 20 minutes.

To serve spoon the dumplings into shallow soup plates; cover with the Blueberry Sauce.

Serve with whipped or heavy cream.

BLUEBERRY COFFEECAKE   *Serves 8 to 10*

1/2 pound   Butter, room temperature

1 cup honey

4 eggs

1 pint sour cream

2 cups flour, whole wheat

2 cups flour, unbleached

2 teaspoons baking soda

2 teaspoons baking powder

2 teaspoons vanilla extract

1-1/2 cups blueberries, fresh, washed, dried

1-1/2 cups sugar, granulated, mixed with

2 tablespoons cinnamon, ground

Heat oven to 350°F. Grease and flour a 9-inch tube pan; set aside.

In a large bowl, cream soft butter; stir in honey, eggs, and sour cream.

In another bowl, sift flour, baking soda, and baking powder together; add to liquids. Add vanilla and mix well.

Into the tube pan, pour half the batter. Cover with a layer of blueberries mixed with half the sugar-cinnamon mix. Pour in remaining batter.

Top with remaining sugar-cinnamon mix.

Bake at 350°F for 50 to 60 minutes. Cool on a rack. Serve warm or cold.

BLUEBERRY BUTTERMILK MUFFINS *Makes 16*

2 cups flour, all purpose

1/2 cup sugar, granulated

2-1/2 teaspoons baking powder

1/2 teaspoon baking soda

1 cup blueberries, fresh or frozen

1 cup buttermilk

1/3 cup vegetable oil

1 egg

As needed - sugar, granulated

Heat oven to 400°F. Grease or paper line muffin tins; set aside.

In a large bowl, mix together flour, sugar, baking powder, and baking soda; fold in blueberries. Set aside.

In another bowl, mix together buttermilk, oil, and egg.

Pour wet ingredients into dry ones; mix gently with a fork until flour disappears. Do not over mix. Batter should be lumpy.

Transfer batter into tins, 3/4 full. Sprinkle each muffin with 1/2 teaspoon sugar.

Bake 25 minutes, or until just golden brown. Serve warm.

BLUEBERRY COBBLER   *Serves 4 to 6*

6 tablespoons butter, unsalted

1/4 cup flour, all purpose

1/4 cup + 1 tablespoon sugar, granulated

1 teaspoon baking powder

1/4 teaspoon salt

1/4 cup milk

2 cups blueberries, fresh, washed, dried

Heat oven to 350°F. Adjust oven rack to lower-middle position. Put butter in an 8-inch square pan; set in oven to melt.

In a small bowl, whisk flour, 1/4 cup sugar, baking powder, and salt.

Add milk; whisk just until ingredients are incorporated.

When butter is melted, remove pan from oven. Pour batter into pan without stirring it into the butter.

Arrange fruit over batter. Sprinkle with remaining tablespoon sugar.

Bake in 350°F for about 40 to 50 minutes. Great served warm.

Apples

In the 1830s, apples were a popular food. Apple pies were eaten for breakfast, lunch, and dinner. Cider, made from the abundant supply of apples, was a popular and favored drink because water supplies were of questionable safety. Consequently, cider served as the drink of the day.

Farmers usually had one or more barrels of cider on the farm. One was to drink when fresh, the other to harden, and enjoy on special occasions. Distilled cider resulted in the famous Pine Barrens applejack (apple brandy), more commonly called "Jersey Lightning," a local favorite. The applejack or "Jersey Lightening" was aged in wooden casks then either bottled or sold in stoneware jugs.

Overindulgence of "Jersey Lightning" often resulted in a condition called "apple palsy." Fortunately or unfortunately during this time, the temperance movement flourished. Many apple trees were cut down by prohibition officers. Applejack Lane in Chatsworth was named after that favorite drink. Today no apple trees can be found here.

APPLE CIDER POUND CAKE *Serves 8 to 10*

Cake

3 cups sugar, granulated

1-1/2 cups butter

6 eggs

3 cups flour, all purpose

1/2 teaspoon salt

1/2 teaspoon baking powder

1 teaspoon cinnamon, ground

1/2 teaspoon nutmeg, ground

1/2 teaspoon allspice, ground

1/4 teaspoon cloves, ground

1 cup apple cider

1 teaspoon vanilla extract

Icing

1/2 cup sugar, granulated

1/4 cup butter

1/4 cup buttermilk

1/2 teaspoon vanilla, extract

1/4 teaspoon baking soda

Heat oven to 325°F. Grease a 10-inch tube pan; set aside.

In a large bowl, cream sugar and butter. Add eggs, one at a time; mix well.

In a large bowl, combine all dry ingredients; mix well and set aside.

In a small bowl, combine cider and vanilla. Set aside.

To sugar-butter mixture, add dry ingredients alternating with cider mixture. Mix until well blended. Spoon mixture into tube cake pan.
Bake in 325°F oven for 1 hour and 10 minutes, or until cake tester comes out clean. Cool on a rack.

Icing
In a saucepan, combine all icing ingredients. Bring to a boil, reduce heat, and simmer for 10 minutes.

When cake is warm, drizzle 1/3 of icing over cake.

Serve remaining icing over individual pieces when served.

APPLE CIDER GLAZED HAM   *Serves 6*
1 4- to 5- pound ham

2 cups apple cider

2 cinnamon sticks, 4-inches long

16 cloves, whole

16 allspice, whole

1/4 cup honey

4 teaspoons cornstarch

As needed apples, red and green, sliced thin

Bake ham as usual.

In a medium saucepan, combine apple cider and spices; bring to a boil. Reduce heat; simmer for 15 minutes. Remove spices; discard.

To cider, add honey and cornstarch. Over medium heat, cook until mixture thickens, stirring constantly.
Thirty minutes before ham is done, begin glazing. Fifteen minutes later, remove ham from oven, arrange apple slices on top. Continue to bake and glaze until ham is done.

APPLE CIDER PIE   *Serves 8*

2 cups apple cider

1 6-inch cinnamon stick

8 cups apples, cooking, peeled, sliced

1 tablespoon lemon juice (optional)

1 cup raisins (or dried mixed fruit bits)

1/3 cup sugar, granulated

2 cups flour, all purpose

1/2 teaspoon salt

2/3 cup shortening

2 tablespoons butter

As needed milk

2 tablespoons honey

1 tablespoon cornstarch

Heat oven to 375°F.

Apple Cider Pastry

In a medium bowl, combine flour and salt. Cut in 2/3 cup shortening until pieces are size of peas.

Sprinkle 1 tablespoon cold apple cider over part of mixture; toss with fork. Push to side. Repeat until all is moistened using 6 to 7 tablespoons of cider. Refrigerate until needed.

Filling

In a large pot, bring apple cider and cinnamon stick to boiling. Boil gently, uncovered, 20 minutes, or until reduced to 1 cup. Strain through a cheesecloth-lined sieve. Discard cinnamon stick. Set aside.

In a large pan, combine apples with lemon juice. Add 2 tablespoons reserved cider mixture. Over medium heat, cook, covered, 4 to 5 minutes, or until apples are tender but not soft. Remove from heat and add raisins; toss.

In a small bowl, combine 2 tablespoons sugar and flour; mix well. Stir into apple mixture.

Pastry

Remove pastry from refrigerator. Divide in half. On a lightly floured surface, roll dough into a 12-inch circle to fit into a 9-inch pie plate. Trim pastry even with rim.

Add filling to pastry; dot with 1 tablespoon butter. Roll remaining pastry into a 12-inch circle. Place on top of filling. Trim to one-half inch beyond edge. Seal and flute edge high. Brush with milk. Sprinkle with a little sugar.

Cover edge of pie with foil. Bake at 375°F for 25 minutes. Remove foil; bake an additional 20 minutes more, or until crust is golden. Cool.

Apple Cider Sauce
In a small saucepan, combine remaining cider mixture, remaining butter, honey, and cornstarch. Cook until bubbly; cook 2 minutes more.

Serve pie with ice cream and warm Apple Cider Sauce.

FRIED APPLES *Serves 6*

2 quarts apples, firm (Granny Smiths are good), peeled, sliced

2 tablespoons butter, melted

1/3 cup sugar, granulated

1-1/2 cups apple cider

3/4 cup brown sugar, packed firm

1 tablespoon butter

2 tablespoons cornstarch

2 tablespoons raisins

In a large skillet in the melted butter, add apple slices. Cover and simmer for 5 minutes.

Add sugar. Flip apples over, cover, and simmer until tender but not mushy. Remove to serving dish.

To skillet, add apple cider, brown sugar, butter, cornstarch, and raisins. Cook until slightly thickened; add apples.

Great served with ham!

Is it a grunt or a buckle? Just what is a grunt? Our research reveals that grunts are generally made with berries topped by a biscuit-like dough. Buckles are often described as a coffee cake of sorts loaded with fruit and only enough batter to hold the fruit together. The topping is usually crumbly. Both are delicious! Apple Grunt is great but be sure to try this recipe with other fruits too.

APPLE GRUNT   *Serves 6 to 8*

Topping
1/3 cup brown sugar

1 tablespoon flour, all purpose

1/2 teaspoon cinnamon, ground

2 tablespoons butter

In a small bowl, combine ingredients and mix to a crumbly consistency; set aside.

Cake
3 tablespoons butter

1/2 cup sugar, granulated

1 egg

1-1/4 cups flour, all purpose

1 teaspoon baking powder

1/2 teaspoon baking soda

1/2 teaspoon salt

1/2 cup buttermilk

2-1/2 cups apples, peeled, sliced thin

Heat oven to 425°F oven. Grease and flour an 8-inch square pan; set aside.

In a large bowl, cream together butter and sugar; beat in egg.

In another bowl, sift together flour, baking powder, baking soda, and salt. Add to creamed mixture alternately with buttermilk; mix well.

Fold in apples. Transfer mixture to the prepared pan. Top with brown sugar mixture.

Bake at 425°F for 30 minutes. Serve warm!

APPLE PANDOWDY   *Serves 8-10*

This old time dish enjoyed frequently by New Gretna residents was a specialty of Monica Walker Kalm and Claire Kalm Allen. Served frequently when friends and neighbors gathered, these ladies are fondly remember for this Amagnet from the stove. (Bass River Gazette 9, Jan-Mar, 2001)

4 cups flour, all purpose, sifted

6 teaspoons baking powder

1 teaspoon salt

3 tablespoons sugar, granulated

3 cups milk

1-1/3 cups shortening

1 cup brown sugar

To taste cinnamon, ground

12 apples, large, peeled, sliced

Heat oven to 400°F. Grease a 12x16-inch pan; set aside.

Place apples in greased pan; cover with brown sugar and sprinkling of cinnamon.

In a large bowl, make biscuit dough by combining flour, baking powder, salt, sugar, and shortening. Mix until crumbly.

Add milk; mix well until a dough forms. Dough should be thin enough to cover apples. Cover apples with dough.

Bake at 400°F for about 30 minutes, until apples are tender and crust is nicely browned.

This is a dish for a crowd! Great for a church supper.

APPLE SLUMP *Serves 4*

6 cups apples, peeled, cored, sliced thin

1 cup sugar, granulated

1 teaspoon cinnamon, ground

1/2 cup water

1-1/2 cups glour, all purpose

1/4 teaspoon salt

1-1/2 teaspoons baking powder

1/2 cup milk

As needed cream

In a large saucepan combine apple slices, sugar, and water. Cover with tightly fitting lid. Heat to a boil.

In a bowl, sift together flour, salt, and baking powder. Stir in enough milk to make a soft dough.

Drop dough from a tablespoon onto apple mixture. Cover tightly and cook over low heat for 30 minutes.

Serve warm with cream.

APPLESAUCE CAKE   *Serves 6 to 8*

1-1/2 cups flour, all purpose
1 teaspoon baking soda
Pinch salt
1 teaspoon cinnamon, ground
1 teaspoon cloves, ground
1/2 cup shortening
3/4 cup brown sugar, packed firm
1 egg
1 cup applesauce
1 cup nuts, chopped
1 cup raisins
1/2 cup dates, pitted, chopped
As needed confectioners sugar

Heat oven to 350°F. Grease a loaf pan. Set aside.

In a bowl, sift together flour, baking soda, salt, cinnamon, and cloves; set aside.

In a large mixing bowl, beat shortening until soft; add sugar, a little at a time, mixing until smooth. Beat in egg.

Alternately add flour mixture and applesauce. Fold in nuts, raisins, and dates.

Add batter to prepared pan and bake at 350°F for 50 to 60 minutes, or until cake pulls away from sides of pan. Cool several minutes before turning out onto a cake rack. Dust with confectioners sugar before serving.

FRESH APPLE CAKE   *Serves 6 to 8*

1 cup   vegetable oil

2 cups sugar, granulated

2 eggs

1 teaspoon salt

1 teaspoon vanilla extract

2 teaspoons baking powder

1 teaspoon cinnamon, ground

2-1/2 cups flour, all purpose

2 cup walnuts, chopped

3 cups apples, peeled, diced

Heat oven to 370°F. Grease and flour a 9x13-inch pan; set aside.

In a mixing bowl, combine oil, sugar, eggs, salt, and vanilla; set aside.

In another bowl, sift flour with baking powder and cinnamon. Add to oil mixture, stirring well.

Fold in nuts and apples.

Pour batter into prepared pan. Bake at 370°F for 1 hour or until toothpick inserted comes out clean. Cool on a rack. Best served warm.

APPLE BUTTER   *Makes 4 pints*

3 quarts cider, sweet

8 pounds apples, peeled, cored, sliced

2-1/2 cups brown sugar, packed firm

2 teaspoons cloves, ground

2 teaspoons cinnamon, ground

1 teaspoon allspice, ground

1/2 teaspoon salt

In a large pot, cook cider over low heat, about 30 minutes, or until it is reduced in half.

Add apples to cider. Cook over low heat until very tender. Stir frequently.

Put apple mixture through a sieve; return puree to pot.

Add sugar, spices, and salt. Over low heat, cook, stirring continuously, until Apple Butter thickens.

Pour into sterilized jars and seal securely. Enjoy!

APPLESAUCE   *Makes 5 to 6 cups*

10 apples, large, peeled, cored, sliced thin

1 cup water

1 cup sugar, granulated

Garnish cinnamon, ground

In a large pot, combine apples and water. Over low heat cook, covered, for 15 minutes, stirring occasionally.

Remove pan from heat. If desired, put apples through a sieve or blend with an electric blender to make a smooth sauce. Apples can be left chunky, too.

Add sugar and return to heat. Cook 5 minutes longer.

Cool but do not chill. Garnish generously with cinnamon. Serve plain or with cold, heavy cream.

APPLE PIE   *Makes one 9-inch pie*

1 pastry for 2-crust pie

4 cups apples, peeled, sliced thin

1 cup sugar, granulated

1/4 teaspoon salt

1/2 teaspoon cinnamon, ground

1/2 lemon, rind grated

1 tablespoon lemon juice

As needed butter

As needed cream

Heat oven to 450°F. Line a 9-inch pie pan with pastry. Refrigerate until needed.

In a large bowl, combine and mix apples, sugar, salt, cinnamon, lemon rind, and lemon juice.

Inside chilled pastry shell, arrange rows of apple slices about 1/2 inch from edge. Work toward center until shell is covered. Pile remaining slices on top. Dot with butter.

Cover pie with top crust. Seal edges securely and crimp. Slash crust in several places.

Bake at 450°F for 10 minutes. Reduce heat to 350°F and bake 30 to 35 minutes more.

Five minutes before pie has finished baking, brush top crust with cream and sprinkle generously with sugar.
Serve warm or at room temperature with cheddar cheese or ice cream!

Pie Pastry   *Makes two 9-inch crusts*

2 cups flour, all purpose

1 teaspoon salt

2/3 cup shortening

5-6 tablespoons water, icy cold

In a bowl, sift flour and salt together.

With a pastry blender, cut in shortening until mixture looks crumbly.

Sprinkle water over mixture. Mix lightly with a fork, then work pastry with your hands until it forms a ball. Chill thoroughly.

Divide dough in half. Roll out one portion at a time on a lightly floured board.

Start at center and roll toward the edge, using light strokes.

When dough is 1/3-inch thick, line a 9-inch pie pan, pressing dough to bottom and sides. Refrigerate both parts while preparing filling.

Roll out second half as before. Place over filling, seal edges, crimp, and slash in several spots.

APPLE & GREEN TOMATO PIE *Makes one 9-inch pie*

1 pastry for 2-crust pie

3 apples, medium, tart, peeled, sliced

2 cups green tomatoes, sliced

1/2 cup sugar, granulated

1/2 cup sugar, brown

1 teaspoon cinnamon, ground

1/4 teaspoon nutmeg, ground

2 tablespoons flour, all purpose

1 tablespoon lemon juice

1 tablespoons butter

1 tablespoon cream or melted butter

Heat oven to 450°F. Line a 9-inch pan with pastry; set aside.

In a large bowl, combine sugar, spices, and flour. Mix lightly.

Gently fold in apples, tomatoes, and lemon juice.

Fill pie shell with mixture. Add top crust. Seal and crimp edges.

Brush top crust with melted butter or cream. Slash in several places.

Bake at 450°F for about 15 minutes, or until crust is golden brown. Reduce heat to 350°F and bake for a total of 1 hour. Cool before serving.

MULLED BUTTERY CIDER   *Serves 6*

1/2 cup brown sugar

1 orange, juice of

1 lemon, juice of

2 quarts apple cider

4 cloves, whole

2 cinnamon sticks, 4-inches long

1 tablespoon allspice, whole

3 tablespoons butter

In a large saucepan, combine sugar and juices; over low heat, cook until syrupy.

Add cider, cloves, cinnamon sticks, and allspice; simmer, covered, for 1 hour.

Strain to remove spices.
To serve, pour into mugs and float 1/2 tablespoon butter on top.

Treats

Molasses was commonly available and used to sweeten many dishes. Children of the pines needed sweet treats such as children do today. Molasses Taffy, a simple candy, was a favorite.

MOLASSES TAFFY

2 cups molasses

1 cup brown sugar

2 tablespoons butter

2 teaspoons cream of tartar

1 teaspoon baking soda

1 tablespoon vinegar, cider or white

In a heavy-bottomed saucepan, combine molasses, brown sugar, and butter; boil for 20 minutes or until a candy thermometer reads 257°F. When done, add cream of tartar, baking soda, and vinegar. Mix well.

Pour the hot candy out into a well-buttered plate with high sides. Let cool. As the edges cool, push them into the center so the mass cools evenly.

When the candy is fairly firm and no longer warm, begin pulling it. Butter your fingers and pick up a big, sticky piece of candy and stretch it with your finger tips. Double it over and stretch it again. Do this until the candy is pale and glossy and lies in a nice rope when put down.

Form into a rope about twice the width of a pencil and put onto a buttered plate or waxed paper. Cut into 1-inch pieces and let harden before wrapping. Delicious!

BUTTERMILK BISCUITS   *Makes 12 to 15*

2 cups flour, all purpose

1 teaspoon baking soda

1 teaspoon baking powder

1 teaspoon salt

1 cup buttermilk (or sour cream)

Heat oven to 425°F.

In a large bowl, sift flour, salt, baking powder, and baking soda together.

Add buttermilk (or sour cream); blend with fork until you have a soft dough. Place dough on a lightly floured board and roll 1/2 inch thick.

Cut with a biscuit cutter, place on a cookie sheet and bake at 425°F for 12 to 15 minutes, or until lightly browned.

Serve piping hot with butter, honey, or jam.

SNICKERDOODLES   *Makes 32*

1/2 pound butter, unsalted, softened

1-1/2 cups + 2 tablespoons sugar, granulated

2 eggs, large, beaten light

2-3/4 cups flour, all purpose

2 teaspoons cream of tartar

1 teaspoon baking soda

1/4 teaspoon salt

2 teaspoons cinnamon, ground

In a large bowl, combine butter and 1-1/2 cups sugar; mix until light and fluffy.

Beat in eggs.

Add flour, cream of tartar, baking soda, and salt; mix until a smooth dough forms.

Cover dough with plastic wrap and refrigerate for about 1 hour or overnight. Heat oven to 350°F.

In a small bowl, combine remaining sugar and cinnamon.

Scoop tablespoon-size balls of dough and roll into a ball. Roll in cinnamon-sugar mix.

On a cookie sheet, arrange balls of dough about 2 inches apart.

Bake at 350°F for about 20 minutes, or until golden on the

bottom. Leave cookies on the sheet for about 2 minutes, then transfer to a rack to cool. Enjoy!

WILD (FOX) GRAPE JELLY
(Also called Alexander Grape or Black Grape)

Wash and pick over grapes, discarding overripe and rotten fruit. Make sure that about 10% of grapes are green (un-ripe). These grapes have the highest pectin content which is responsible for the jelling process. The best jelly grapes are slightly tart.

Drain grapes and place pot on stove to boil; stir occasion-ally so that grapes do not burn.

When grapes are slightly soft, crush with a potato masher. Boil the entire batch for 30 minutes, stirring all the time.

Filter mixture through multilayered (4) cheesecloth. Allow juice to drip overnight. Do not squeeze or jelly will be cloudy.

Measure juice. Place in large pot over high heat and bring to a boil; boil for 5 minutes.

Add sugar, amount equal to that of juice; stir frequently.

Bring to a boil. Skim foam from surface; discard.

Test jelly to see if it is done. Test twice:
(1) Dip a spoon in liquid, pull out, and hold sideways. If jelly sheets and two drops hang together from the side of the

spoon, it's done.

(2) Pour a little juice into a plate to see if jelly "wrinkles." If so, it's done.

Pour jelly into clean, dry glasses, seal, and store Enjoy!

Desserts

MUSTER DAY GINGERBREAD   *Serves 6 to 8*

What is Muster Day? This was the day when local men gathered to train for military service; it is a gathering, a convening. Gingerbread was frequently eaten.

1/3 cup lard
1/2 cup brown sugar, packed firm
1/2 cup molasses
1 egg
2 cups flour, all purpose
1 teaspoon baking soda
3/4 teaspoon ginger, ground
3/4 teaspoon cinnamon, ground
1/4 teaspoon cloves, ground
1/4 teaspoon salt
1/2 cup water, boiling

Heat oven to 350°F. Grease an 8-1/2 x 4-1/2 x 2-1/2- inch loaf pan. Set aside.

In a large bowl, combine lard and brown sugar; cream until light.

Add molasses and egg; beat well.In a separate bowl, stir together flour, soda, spices, and salt. Add to the creamed mixture alternately with the boiling water, beating after each addition.

To loaf pan, add batter and bake at 350°F for about 50 minutes. Cool a few minutes before removing from pan, and wrap. This cake tastes even better the next day.

OLD FASHIONED GINGERBREAD *Serves 12*

2-1/2 cups flour, all purpose

2 teaspoons baking soda

2 teaspoons ginger, ground

1-1/2 teaspoons cinnamon, ground

1/2 teaspoon salt

1 egg, large

1/2 cup dark brown sugar, packed

1 cup oil, canola or corn

1 cup molasses

1/2 cup applesauce

1/2 cup buttermilk

Heat oven to 350°F. Lightly oil an 8 x12-1/2 inch baking pan.

In a bowl, whisk flour, baking soda, ginger, cinnamon, and salt. Set aside.

In a large bowl, beat egg, sugar, and oil until thick and creamy. Beat in applesauce and molasses.

With a rubber spatula, gently mix dry ingredients and buttermilk into the egg mixture, making 3 additions of dry ingredients and 2 additions of buttermilk. Do not over mix!

Scrape batter into prepared pan. Bake at 350°F for 40 minutes, or until a skewer inserted in the center comes out clean. Let cool slightly in the pan on a wire rack.

PINEAPPLE UPSIDE DOWN CAKE

Topping

3/4 stick butter

1/2 cup brown sugar

1-8 ounce can pineapple slices, drained; juice reserved.

In a 9-inch baking pan (cast iron is best), melt butter. Add brown sugar. Arrange pineapple slices; set aside.

Dough

1-3/4 cups flour, all purpose

1/4 teaspoon salt

2-1/2 teaspoons baking powder

1 cup sugar, granulated

1/2 cup butter

1/2 cup milk

1 egg

1 teaspoon vanilla

1/2 cup pineapple juice

Heat oven to 350°F.

In a bowl, combine flour, salt, and baking powder. Whisk together; set aside.

In a large bowl, combine sugar and butter; mix well. Add milk, egg, vanilla, and pineapple juice. Mix thoroughly.

To this mixture add flour mixture; mix well. Pour batter on top of fruit.

Bake at 350°F for 35 to 40 minutes. Remove pan from oven and immediately turn upside down on a plate; allow to cool. Remove pan and serve. For best flavor, serve warm.

MINCED FRUIT PIES   *Makes 12*

2 cups flour, all purpose

1 cup butter, unsalted

1/2 teaspoon salt

1 egg yolk, beaten

4 tablespoons water, iced

1 tablespoon vinegar, white

1 cup fruit, minced (apples, peaches, pears)

1egg white, whisked

As needed confectioners sugar

Heat oven to 425°F. Grease muffin tins; set aside.

In a large bowl, combine flour, butter and salt; mix well.

In a small bowl, beat together egg yolk, iced water, and vinegar. Add to dry ingredients; mix. Form mixture into a ball (mixture will be very soft) and chill until firm.

Between two pieces of waxed paper, roll out dough until thin. Cut 12 rounds with a 4-inch cookie cutter and 12 rounds with a 3-inch cutter.

Fit the 4-inch rounds into muffin tins; fill each with rounded tablespoon of minced fruit. Wet each pastry edge, cover with 3-inch pastry round and seal by pressing down lightly around the edges. Prick each pie several times with tines of fork; Brush with whisked egg white.

Bake at 425°F for about 10 to 15 minutes, or until golden. Serve warm for best flavor.

STRAWBERRY-RHUBARB PIE *Serves 6 to 8*

Filling

2-1/2 cups strawberries, hulled, halved

2-1/2 cups rhubarb, cut into 1-inch pieces

3/4 cup brown sugar, light, packed

1/4 cup maple syrup

4 tablespoons flour, all purpose

1/2 teaspoon nutmeg, ground

1/8 teaspoon salt

2 tablespoons butter

In a large bowl, combine strawberries and rhubarb with sugar, maple syrup, flour, nutmeg, salt, and butter; mix well. Set aside while you make pie crust.

Crust

2-1/2 cups flour, all purpose

1 teaspoon salt

7 tablespoons butter, chilled

7 tablespoons shortening, chilled

5 to 8 tablespoons water, cold

Heat oven to 425°F. In a large bowl, combine flour and salt. Cut butter in small pieces and add with shortening to flour. Blend rapidly so that butter and shortening do not soften, until mixture forms lumps the size of coarse crumbs.

Blend in 5 tablespoons water. Add more if needed. Remove dough from bowl and blend with heel of hand. Wrap dough in waxed paper and chill for at least 2 hours.

Cut dough in half. Roll out half of it 1/4-inch thick; line pie pan. Add filling.

Roll out remaining dough and cover pie. Trim overhang to 3/4-inch. Fold under bottom crust's overlap and flute. Pierce top crust with a fork to form vent holes.

Bake 10 minutes at 425°F, then reduce heat to 350°F and bake another 40 to 45 minutes, until nicely browned. Serve at room temperature, topped with whipped cream, if desired.

MIXED FRUIT PANCAKES *Makes ten 6-inch pancakes*

1-3/4 cups flour, all purpose

1/4 cup sugar, granulated

2 tablespoons baking powder

4 tablespoons butter, melted

1 egg

1-1/2 cups milk

1/2 cup blueberries

1/2 cup peaches, sliced thin

1/2 cup apple, chopped fine

1/2 cup banana, sliced

As needed syrup

In a large bowl, combine flour, sugar, and baking powder. Stir in butter, egg, and milk; beat to a smooth consistency. Gently fold in fruit.

Pour or ladle 1/3 cup batter onto lightly oiled griddle. Cook until bubbles appear dry. Flip pancake and cook other side. Repeat until all batter is used up.

Serve pancakes with syrup of choice.

BREAD PUDDING   *Serves 4 to 6*

As great cooks go, Lizzie (Elizabeth) Allen Gerew was one of the best. Her cakes were featured at New Gretna birth-

day parties. *She was well known for her delicious Bread Pudding. (Bass River Gazette 8, Sep-Oct, 2000)*

1 quart milk

2 tablespoons butter

4 eggs, separated

3/4 cupsugar, granulated

1 teaspoon vanilla extract

4 cups bread, cut into cubes.

Heat oven to 375°F. Butter a 1-1/2 or 2 quart baking dish; set aside.

In a large pot, heat milk and butter just to boiling. Place in a large bowl and add bread cubes.

In a separate large bowl, beat 4 egg yolks until fluffy; add sugar and vanilla.

Add egg yolk mixture to milk-bread mixture; mix well. Pour into buttered baking dish that has been set in a pan of water.

Bake at 375°F until the pudding is set, about 1-1/2 hours.

While the pudding is baking, in a large bowl, beat 4 egg whites until stiff. Add 1/2 cup sugar and beat until very stiff. Place egg whites (meringue) on top of baked pudding. Return to oven and bake until golden brown, 12 to 15 minutes. Serve warm or cold.

COCONUT LAYER CAKE

This favorite was made frequently by Janet Parker White who lived in the New Gretna area for many years. The cake, a New Gretna favorite, was made by her family for many generations. It was served on very special occasions for special people. (Bass River Gazette 15, Jul-Dec, 2003)

2 cups cake flour (sift before measuring)

1-1/2 cups sugar, granulated

2/3 cup milk

1/2 cup shortening (Crisco7)

1 teaspoon salt

3 teaspoons baking powder

2 egg yolks

2 eggs

1/2 cup milk

1/2 teaspoon lemon extract

As needed coconut, shredded

Heat oven to 375°F. Grease two 9-inch layer pans; line with waxed paper; set aside.

In a large bowl, blend vigorously flour, sugar, milk, shortening, and salt. Stir in baking powder.

Add eggs, egg yolks, milk, and lemon extract. Mix well for 2 minutes.

Pour batter into pans. Bake at 375°F for 25 to 30 minutes. Cool on rack.

Frost with Snow Frosting and sprinkle top and sides with coconut.

Snow Frosting

1 egg white

3/4 cup sugar, granulated

3 tablespoons water

1 teaspoon corn syrup, light

1/2 teaspoon vanilla

In the top of a double boiler, combine egg white, sugar, salt, water, and corn syrup. Beat for about 1 minute, or until thoroughly mixed.

Over rapidly boiling water, cook, beating constantly for 4 minutes, or until frosting will stand up in peaks. With a spatula, occasionally stir frosting up from bottom and sides of pan.

Remove from boiling water. Add vanilla and beat 1 minute or until frosting is thick enough to spread.

Frost cooked cake. Apply coconut. Serve!

HOT MILK CAKE   *Serves 8 to 10*

Another Lizzie Gerew specialty! (Bass River Gazette 8, Sep-Dec, 2000)

4 eggs

2 cups sugar, granulated

2 cups cake flour

3 teaspoons baking powder

1 teaspoon vanilla extract

1 cup milk

2 tablespoons butter, unsalted

Heat oven to 350°F. Grease and flour two 9-inch cake pans; set aside.

In a saucepan, heat milk and butter; do not boil.

In a small bowl, beat one whole egg. Transfer to a large bowl. Beat yolks of remaining 3 eggs separately and add them to the large bowl. To large bowl, add sugar and continue beating.

Combine flour and baking powder. Add alternately with hot milk to eggs; add vanilla extract.

Transfer batter to cake pans. Bake at 350°F for 45 to 60 minutes. Take care not to over-bake. If desired, ice with favorite icing.

PEACH POUND CAKE   *Serves 8 to 10*

3 cups sugar, granulated

1 cup butter

6 eggs

1 teaspoon vanilla extract

1/2 teaspoon almond extract

1/4 teaspoon baking soda

1/2 teaspoon salt

3 cups flour

1/2 cup sour cream

2 cups peaches, fresh, peeled, chopped

Heat oven to 350°F. Grease and flour a 10-inch tube pan; set aside.

In a large bowl, combine butter and sugar; cream until light and fluffy.

Add eggs, one at a time; mix until well blended.

Stir in vanilla and almond extract.

In another bowl, combine flour, salt, and baking soda; add to creamed mixture mixing gently.
Fold in sour cream and peaches.

Pour batter in tube pan; bake in 350°F for about 70 minutes. Test with cake tester.

Let cake cool in pan for 5 minutes; turn out to cool completely. Serve plain or with whipped cream.

This cake is frequently made by Ethel Estlow and her friend Alma who acquired the recipe from friends. Try it - it's exceptional!

Blackberries

Blackberries, although not a native fruit, soon grew wild in the pines. Often considered a nuisance today, blackberries are cultivated in no other part of the world. In the 1830s blackberries were found worth cultivating here. Although used primarily for medicinal purposes (Blackberry Syrup for cholera and summer complaint), blackberries eventually found their way into cookbooks. Blackberry pie is a favorite today.

These delicious berries can also be used for cobbles, pies, jam, jelly, and crisps.

BLACKBERRY PIE *Makes one 9-inch pie*

1 pastry for 2-crust pie

4 cups blackberries, fresh, washed, dried

3 tablespoons flour, all purpose

1 tablespoon lemon juice

1 tablespoon butter

Heat oven to 450°F. Line a 9-inch pie pan with pastry. Chill while preparing fruit.

In a bowl, combine blackberries with flour and lemon juice.

Mix gently. Spoon fruit mixture into pie shell. Dot with butter.

Cover with top crust. Seal edges, crimp, and slash top in several places.

Bake at 450°F for 15 minutes. Reduce heat to 350EF and bake 35 to 40 minutes, more, or until brown. Serve warm!

BLACKBERRY-APPLE COBBLER   *Serves 4 to 6*

2 cups blackberries, washed, drained

2 cups apples, tart, peeled, sliced

1/2 cup brown sugar, light

1/2 teaspoon cinnamon, ground

2 tablespoons water

2 cups flour, all purpose

2 teaspoons baking powder

1/4 teaspoon salt

3 tablespoons sugar, granulated

1/2 cup butter, unsalted, softened

1 egg, beaten

1/2 cup milk

Heat oven to 425°F. Grease a 2-quart baking dish; set aside.

In a saucepan, combine apples, brown sugar, and cinnamon with 2 tablespoons water. Over low heat, cook until apples are barely tender. Remove from heat. Gently fold in blackberries and pour into baking dish; set aside.

In a large bowl, combine flour, baking powder, salt, and granulated sugar. With a fork or pastry cutter, mix in butter until the mixture resembles coarse cornmeal.

Add the egg and milk, stirring until mixed. Drop dough by spoonfuls over the fruit.

Bake at 425°F for approximately 30 minutes, or until lightly browned. Serve warm with a scoop of vanilla ice cream.

BLACKBERRY CRISP   *Serves 6*

Crust
1 cup flour, all purpose
1 cup sugar, granulated
1 teaspoon baking powder
1 egg, beaten

Filling
2 tablespoons flour, all purpose
3/4 cup sugar, granulated
4 to 5 cups blackberries, fresh or frozen
1/4 cup butter, unsalted, melted

Heat oven to 375°F. Butter an 8x8x2-inch glass baking dish; set aside.

Topping

In a medium bowl, combine flour, sugar, and baking powder; whisk together.

In the center of the dry ingredients, make a well; blend in egg, mixing until the topping is crumbly; set aside.

Filling

In a small bowl, combine flour and sugar; set aside.

In a large bowl, place blackberries; sprinkle with flour and sugar mix. Toss gently to evenly coat the blackberries.

Transfer berry mixture to the baking dish and sprinkle topping overberries. Drizzle melted butter evenly over the topping. Place baking dish on a baking tray in case of spillovers.

Bake at 375°F for 45 minutes. Cool on a rack until just warm.

Vegetables

Local crops provided delicacies such as pies of apples, blackberries, and pumpkins. Other dishes from garden produce were baked beans, coleslaw, onions, succotash, fried tomatoes, cornbread, sweet potatoes, and red beet eggs. Potatoes, white and sweet, were grown in home gardens and used in many dishes. White potatoes were not commonly used until the 19th century. Other vegetables commonly grown include lima beans, corn, onions, cabbage, and beets.

OLD FASHIONED BAKED LIMAS   *Serves 6 to 8*

2 cups lima beans, dried

1/4 pound bacon, fried crisp or left over ham

1 onion, medium, chopped

1/4 cup molasses

2 tablespoons ketchup or chili sauce

2 tablespoons brown sugar

2 teaspoons salt (if desired)

1 teaspoon mustard, dry

1 cup tomato or V-8 juice

Heat oven to 250°F.

In a large pot, cover beans with water and soak overnight. In the morning simmer for 30 minutes. Add additional water if needed. Drain but save liquid.

In a large baking dish, make alternate layers of beans, bacon, and onions.

In a bowl, combine remaining ingredients; mix well. Pour over beans to cover. Use reserved liquid now if needed.

Cover baking dish and bake at 250°F degrees for 4 to 6 hours, or until beans are tender. Uncover during the last 30 minutes to brown the top. Serve hot!

SWEET POTATO MUFFINS   *Makes 12*

1 sweet potato, large, peeled, cut into chunks*

1-1/2 cups flour, all purpose

1/2 teaspoon salt

1/2 teaspoon cinnamon, ground

1/2 teaspoon nutmeg, ground

1/8 teaspoon cloves, ground

1 egg, large

1/2 cup applesauce (or fruit puree)

1/2 cup sugar, granulated

2 tablespoons oil, canola or corn

1 teaspoon vanilla extract

*One cup pureed canned sweet potato can replace the fresh potato.

Heat oven to 350°F. Lightly oil 12 muffin cups; set aside.

In a saucepan of boiling water, cook sweet potato until very tender, 10 to 15 minutes. Drain and let cool. Puree sweet potato until smooth. Measure out 1 cup, reserving remainder for another use.

In a large bowl, whisk together flour, baking powder, salt, cinnamon, nutmeg, and cloves; set aside.

In a medium bowl, whisk egg, 1 cup sweet potato puree, applesauce, sugar, oil, and vanilla extract until smooth.

In the dry ingredients, make a well. Add sweet potato mixture and stir until just combined.

Divide batter among prepared muffin cups. Bake at 350°F for 15 to 20 minutes, or until tops spring back when touched lightly. Let cool in pan on a wire rack for 5 minutes. Serve warm or at room temperature.

RED CABBAGE   *Serves 4*

2 tablespoons shortening or bacon drippings

1 onion, large, chopped fine

2 apples, pared, cored, diced thin

1 cup water

1/2 cup red wine vinegar

2 tablespoons sugar, granulated

1 teaspoon salt

Dash pepper, ground fresh

1 bay leaf

1 red cabbage, medium, shredded

1 tablespoon flour

In a large heavy saucepan, heat shortening or bacon drippings. Add onion and saute 3 to 4 minutes. Add apple slices and cook for several minutes.

Stir in water, vinegar, sugar, salt, pepper, and bay leaf; bring to a boil.

Add shredded cabbage and stir well. Cover tightly and cook over low heat for 40 to 45 minutes, stirring occasionally.

Just before serving, add flour, stirring occasionally until mixture thickens slightly. Great served with pork, venison, goose, or duck.

ONIONS IN CREAM *Serves 4*

24 onions, white, small, peeled

2 tablespoons butter

2 tablespoons flour, all purpose

1 cup cream, half-and-half

1/2 teaspoon salt

Dash cloves, ground

1/4 cup parsley, chopped

In a large saucepan, cover onions with cold, salted water and bring to a boil. Reduce heat and cook slowly until onions are tender when tested with a fork. Drain thoroughly; set aside.

In a saucepan, melt butter; add flour, a little at a time; stir until smooth. Cook over low heat for several minutes.

Stir in cream and continue cooking, stirring constantly, until sauce is smooth and bubbly.

Remove from heat; stir in salt, cloves, and parsley. Combine with onions.

SUCCOTASH   *Serves 4 to 6*

2 cups lima beans, fresh

2 cups corn, whole kernel (fresh, frozen, or canned)

2 tablespoons butter

1 teaspoon salt

dash pepper, ground fresh

1 teaspoon sugar, granulated

1/2   cup water

1/4 cup cream, heavy

In a medium saucepan in boiling water, cook lima beans until tender; drain. To cooked beans, add corn, butter, salt, pepper, sugar, and water.

Cook over low heat for 10 to 15 minutes. Drain, then add cream. Heat until hot; do not allow to boil.

FRIED TOMATOES

Use firm, almost ripe tomatoes.

Cut into 1/2 inch thick slices. Plan on 2 to 3 slices per person.

Dip each slice into corn meal (or flour) seasoned with salt and pepper. Coat both sides. Set aside.
In a large frying pan, fry bacon until crisp, allowing 2 slices per person. Drain bacon on paper towels; set aside.

To bacon fat, add tomato slices and fry for several minutes on one side until coating is crisp.

When frying more than one panful, wipe out pan (with paper towels), add more fat, and proceed with second batch.

Serve piping hot with bacon.

BOSTON BAKED BEANS   *Serves 10 to 12*

6 cups beans, navy or pea

1 pound salt pork

1 tablespoon mustard, dry

1 tablespoon salt

1 teaspoon black pepper, ground fresh

1 cup molasses

1 onion, small (optional)

An earthenware casserole serves nicely as a bean pot if you don't have one.

In a large pot, cover beans with cold water. Soak overnight. In morning, drain, cover with fresh water. Bring to a boil over low heat; simmer until beans burst. Drain beans.

In another pot, place salt pork in boiling water. Let stand for 5 to 10 minutes. Cut off two thin slices, one to place in bottom of bean pot, dice the other. Score the rind of the remaining piece.

In a bowl, combine and mix dry mustard, salt, pepper, and molasses.

In the bean pot, first place a slice of salt pork then layer alternately beans and molasses mixture, and bits of salt pork. Bury onion in the middle. When the pot is full, push the large piece of salt pork down into the beans with the rind sticking up.

Add boiling water to cover, put on lid, and bake all day at 250°F. Add boiling water as needed.

During the last hour of baking, uncover pot so rind can crisp. Serve piping hot!

YAMS AND APPLES   *Serves 4 to 6*

Heat oven to 350°F. Butter a large baking dish; set aside.

Select four large yams (sweet potatoes). Wash, then bake in 350°F oven until tender. Cool.

While yams are baking, peel 4 tart apples, core, and slice thin.

When cooked and cooled, peel yams, cut into 1/2 inch slices; arrange in alternate layers of yams and apples in baking pan. Sprinkle each layer with sugar and a dash of nutmeg. Dot with butter.

Cover and bake at 350°F for 25 to 30 minutes.

Serve with roast duck, chicken, ham, or game.

PEPPER RELISH

12 green bell peppers

6 red bell peppers

12 onions, small, peeled

2 tablespoons mustard seeds

2 cups sugar, granulated

1 cup water

1 teaspoon salt

3 cups vinegar, cider

Wash peppers; remove core and seeds; grind with onions. Place in a large nonaluminum pot and cover with boiling water. Let stand at least 5 minutes; drain and discard liquid.

To pepper-onion mixture add mustard seed, sugar, water, salt, and vinegar. Boil uncovered for 20 minutes.

Ladle hot relish into hot sterilized jars. Seal. Enjoy!

RED BEET EGGS   *Serves 4*

1 teaspoon mustard, dried

2 tablespoons sugar, granulated

1 teaspoon salt

1/2 cup cider vinegar

1 can (pound) baby beets, cooked

4 eggs, hard cooked, shelled

In a large bowl, mix together sugar, salt, mustard, and vinegar. Bring to a boil. Remove from heat; add beets. Set aside to cool.

When cool, add eggs. Refrigerate overnight. Shake container occasionally so eggs will pick up beet color all over.

Serve beets as a salad. Use eggs as a garnish or serve separately.

COLESLAW WITH COOKED DRESSING *Serves 4*

1 cabbage, green, medium head, shredded

1/2 cup vinegar

1 cup water

1 egg, well beaten

1 teaspoon salt

1 tablespoon cornstarch

3/4 cup sugar

1 tablespoon butter

1 teaspoon celery seeds (optional)

In a small saucepan, combine cornstarch, sugar, vinegar, and salt. Gradually add water and egg; stir until well blended. Over medium heat, bring to a full boil, stirring constantly.

Remove from heat and stir in butter. Cool to room temperature.

In a large bowl, combine cabbage, celery seed, and dressing. Chill before serving. This dressing is also good for potato or macaroni salad. *(A specialty of Ada Applegate Brown).*

CUCUMBER SALAD   *Serves 6*

2 cucumbers, peeled, sliced very thin
1 onion, small, sliced thin
1/2 cup sour cream
1/3 cup vinegar, cider
3/4 teaspoon salt
1/4 teaspoon pepper, ground fresh

In a small bowl, make dressing by combing all ingredients except onions and cucumbers; mix well.

Place cucumbers and onions in a glass or ceramic bowl. Add dressing and toss gently. Don=t make too far in advance of serving time; salad will become soggy.

SPLIT PEA SOUP   *Serves 6*

1-1/2 cups split peas
1 ham bone
1 onion, stuck with 2 cloves
2-3 celery stalks, cut into chunks
1 bay leaf
3-4 carrots, cut into chunks
1/2 cup cream, heavy

In a large pot, cover split peas with water and soak overnight (or use quick-cooking variety); drain, discarding water.

In a stock pot, combine ham bone, onion, celery, bay leaf, carrots, and split peas. Add 2-3 quarts of water.

Bring to a boil, then lower heat, and simmer gently until peas are soft and mushy.

Remove ham bone, then puree soup in a blender or sieve.

Pour soup back into stock pot, add cream, and correct seasoning.

Remove meat from ham bone and add to pot. Bring to a boil but do not cook further. Serve with a crusty bread.

SCALLOPED POTATOES

Select a casserole of a size to feed your group.

Peel potatoes, then slice as thin as possible. Place layer of potatoes in casserole, dust with flour, season with salt and pepper. Add chopped onion, if desired, and dot with butter.

Repeat layers until casserole is full. Add enough milk to cover top layer.

Bake uncovered at 325°F for 1-1/2 hours. The top should brown nicely. Serve piping hot!

Corn

Corn, a native American crop, was a major foodstuff. Eaten fresh or dried, corn was a staple of early diets. The Indians discovered or "invented" corn which was found growing as a wild grass. Indians cultivated it, learning to treat and enhance its particular requirements for best growth. The result was one of the nation's most reliable crops.

Corn, also known as maize, was a life sustaining product in the early days of this country. Ground corn, cornmeal, was prepared for use throughout the year.

In 1835, corn on the cob was first eaten. Corn was also served in breads, porridge, and puddings.

CORNMEAL MUFFINS   *Makes 16*

1 cup cornmeal, yellow

1 cup flour, all purpose

2 teaspoons sugar, granulated

1 teaspoon salt

2 eggs, large, beaten

3 teaspoons baking powder

1 cup milk

1/4 cup butter, unsalted, melted

Heat oven to 425°F. Grease muffin pans; set aside.

In a large bowl, sift together cornmeal, flour, sugar, salt, and baking powder.

Add milk and eggs; beat batter until smooth. Add melted butter and mix. Pour batter into muffin pans filling almost to the top.

Bake at 425°F for 15 to 20 minutes, or until brown and baked through. Check after 10 minutes of baking; if browning too quickly, reduce temperature to 400°F.

Serve warm.

CORN BREAD (CORN PONE) *Makes about 12 servings*

2 cups cornmeal, white

1 teaspoonsalt

1-1/4 teaspoon baking soda

4 tablespoons shortening (or lard)

3/4 cups water, boiling

1/2 cup buttermilk

Heat oven to 350°F.

In a large bowl, sift together cornmeal, salt, and baking soda. With your finger tips, work in shortening until blended.

Pour in boiling water and continue to work the mixture. Gradually add enough buttermilk to make a soft dough, firm enough to be patted into small cakes.

On a hot well-greased iron skillet, place the cakes and bake at 350°F for 35 to 40 minutes. Serve piping hot for best flavor.

CORN BREAD STUFFING *Enough for 12-15lb turkey*

Corn Bread

1-1/2 cups cornmeal

2 cups flour, all purpose

2 tablespoons sugar, granulated

1 teaspoon salt

4 teaspoons baking powder

2 eggs, beaten

2 cups milk

4 tablespoons bacon drippings

Corn Bread

Grease two 9-inch square pans; set aside. Heat oven to 450°F.

In a large bowl, sift cornmeal, flour, sugar, salt, and baking powder.

Stir in eggs, milk, and bacon drippings until well mixed. Spread in baking pans. Bake at 450°F for 30 minutes. Cool and crumble for stuffing.

Stuffing

1 pound sausage

4 onions, medium, chopped fine

4 celery stalks, chopped fine

1/2 teaspoon sage, dried

1 teaspoon salt

Dash pepper, ground fresh

In a large frying pan over low heat, cook sausage until lightly browned; break into small pieces with a fork. Drain excess fat; reserve.

Add crumbled corn bread and mix well. Remove from heat.

In another frying pan in bacon fat, cook onion until limp; add to mixture. Then, add celery and remaining ingredients. Mix well.

Stuff a 12-15 pound turkey. Do not pack tightly.

CORN PUDDING   *Serves 4 to 6*

2 eggs, whole

2 egg whites

2 cups corn kernels (from 4 to 5 ears of corn)

3 tablespoons flour

1 tablespoon sugar, granulated

1 cup milk, skim

1 tablespoon butter, melted

To taste salt and pepper, ground fresh

Heat oven to 325°F. Grease a 1-1/2 quart casserole; set aside.

In a large bowl, beat eggs and egg white until thick; stir in corn. Set aside.

In another bowl combine flour, sugar, salt, and several liberal grindings of pepper. Slowly stir in milk, then butter. Stir mixture into egg-corn mixture.

Pour corn pudding mix into casserole. Bake at 325°F about 1 hour and 20 minutes, or until a knife inserted near center comes out clean. Serve warm.

CORN PANCAKES   *Makes 12 3-inch pancakes*

3/4 cup flour, unbleached

1 tablespoon baking powder

1 teaspoon salt

To taste black pepper, ground fresh

Dash cayenne

1 egg, beaten

1-1/3 cups corn kernels* (about 4 ears); or cream-
style corn kernels

In a bowl, combine flour, baking powder, salt, pepper, and cayenne. Blend in egg. Add corn and mix well; set aside.

Grease a skillet with butter or lard and heat. Drop mixture onto the hot skillet. Cook until golden; turn with spatula and cook second side.

Keep pancakes warm in 200°F oven until all are cooked.

Serve with warm maple syrup. Delicious!

*To make fresh cream-style corn, cut down the center of each row of kernels with a sharp knife; then scrap into a bowl with the back of the knife.

CORN CHOWDER   *Serves 4*

3 salt pork slices, cubed

1 onion, large, sliced

4 potatoes, large, peeled, sliced

2 cups water

6 soda crackers, large

1 cup milk

2 cups corn (fresh, canned, whole kernel)

1 teaspoon salt

Dash paprika

In a large saucepan, fry salt pork until crisp and lightly browned.

Stir in onion; cook until golden. Add potatoes and water. Cook uncovered over low heat until potatoes are tender.

In a bowl, crumble soda crackers; add milk and soak. Add to cooked potatoes.

Add corn, salt, and paprika. Simmer over low heat for 8 to 10 minutes.

INDIAN PUDDING *Serves 6 to 8*

1/4 cup cornmeal

2 cups milk

1/4 cup sugar, granulated

1/8 teaspoon baking soda

1/2 teaspoon salt

1/2 teaspoon ginger, ground

1/2 teaspoon cinnamon, ground

1/4 cup molasses

1 cup milk, cold

As desired cream, whipped

As desired nutmeg, ground

Heat oven to 275°F.

In a large saucepan, heat milk over low heat. Stir in cornmeal, a little at a time, stirring constantly for 15 minutes or until thick. Remove from heat.

In a small bowl, combine sugar, baking soda, salt, ginger, and cinnamon; mix well. Stir into cornmeal mixture.

Add molasses and cold milk, mixing thoroughly.

Pour into a 1-quart casserole. Bake at 275°F for 2 hours. Serve with whipped cream and a sprinkling of nutmeg.

Pumpkin

Pumpkin and other squashes were staple vegetables for Native Americans. The Pilgrims learned to use this versatile vegetable to make everything from soup to pie. Pumpkin Pie was a favorite!

PUMPKIN PIE   *Serves 8*

Crust

1-1/2 cups flour, all purpose

1/2 teaspoon cinnamon, ground

1/4 teaspoon cloves, ground

1/4 teaspoon salt

1/2 cup butter, unsalted, chilled, cut into pieces

4-1/2 tablespoons water, iced

Filling

1 cup sugar, granulated

1/2 cup cream, whipping

1/2 cup milk

1-1/2 cups pumpkin (canned, solid pack)

3 eggs, large

1 egg yolk, large

1/4 cup molasses

1/2 teaspoon cinnamon, ground

1/2 teaspoon nutmeg, ground

1/4 teaspoon cloves, ground

1/4 teaspoon ginger, ground

1/2 teaspoon salt

Heat oven to 400°F.

Crust

In a large bowl, combine flour, cinnamon, cloves, and salt; mix well. Add butter and rub with fingertips until mixture resembles coarse meal.

Add water by tablespoons until dough just begins to come together. Gather dough into ball; flatten into disk, wrap in plastic, and refrigerate at least 15 minutes (can be prepared 1 day ahead if refrigerated).

Turn out dough onto lightly floured surface and knead just until combined.

Filling

In a small heavy saucepan, combine sugar, whipping cream and milk; heat over low heat until sugar dissolves; do not boil.

In a large bowl, combine pumpkin, whole eggs, egg yolk, molasses, spices, and salt; blend well. Gradually whisk in cream mixture. Cover and refrigerate until ready to use.

On a lightly floured surface, roll out dough into a 12-inch circle. Transfer to a 9-inch glass pie plate. Crimp edge decoratively. Freeze 10 minutes.

Line pie crust with foil. Fill with pie weights or dried beans. Bake 15 minutes. Remove foil and beans. Continue to bake until sides are set, piercing with toothpick if crust bubbles, about 10 minutes longer. Transfer crust to rack.

Reduce oven temperature to 350°F.

Spoon filling into crust. Bake until edges are puffed and set but center is still slightly soft, about 50 minutes. Transfer pie to rack and cool. Cover and refrigerate until cold. Serve plain or with whipped cream.

PUMPKIN PIE PERFECT   *Makes 1 9-inch pie*

1 pastry for 1-crust pie

2 cups pumpkin, cooked (fresh, canned, or frozen)

2/3 cup brown sugar, packed firm

2 teaspoons dinnamon, ground

1/2 teaspoon ginger, ground

1/2 teaspoon salt

3/4 cup milk

2 eggs, well beaten

1 cup cream, heavy

1/4 cup brandy

Heat oven to 325°F. Refrigerate pie crust while preparing filling.

In a large bowl, combine pumpkin, sugar, spices and salt. Then beat in milk, eggs, cream, and brandy.

Pour pumpkin mixture into unbaked pie shell.

Bake at 325°F for 1 hour, or until a knife inserted in center comes out dry. Cool.

Serve plain or with whipped cream flavored with ginger. (Beat 1 cup heavy cream and 2 tablespoons candied ginger, minced.)

PUMPKIN BUTTERMILK MUFFINS   *Makes 16-18*
1/2 cup vegetable oil
1 cup sugar, granulated
2 eggs
1 cup pumpkin, pureed or canned
1/3 to 1/2 cup buttermilk
2 cups flour, all purpose
2 teaspoons baking powder
1 teaspoon baking soda
1-1/2 teaspoons cinnamon, ground
1/2 teaspoon allspice, ground
3/4 cup walnuts, chopped
1 cup raisins, yellow

Heat oven to 350°F. Grease or paper line muffin tins; set aside.

In a medium bowl, mix together oil, sugar, eggs, pumpkin, and buttermilk.

Add flour, baking powder, soda, cinnamon and allspice. Mix until batter is smooth. Fold in walnuts and raisins.

Transfer mixture to muffin tins; fill 3/4 full. Bake at 350°F for 30 minutes. For best flavor, serve warm.

PUMPKIN-RAISIN BREAD   *Makes 1 9x5-inch loaf*

2 cups flour, all purpose

1/2 cup milk, dry, nonfat

1 teaspoon cinnamon, ground

1 teaspoon baking powder

1/2 teaspoon baking soda

1/2 teaspoon salt

1/2 teaspoon nutmeg, grated fresh

2 egg whites, large, lightly beat

1 egg, large, lightly beaten

1 cup brown sugar, light, packed

1/4 cup vegetable oil

1 cup raisins

Heat oven to 350°F. Lightly oil a 9x5-inch loaf pan; set aside.

In a mixing bowl, whisk flour, dry milk, cinnamon, baking powder, baking soda, salt, and nutmeg until well blended; set aside.

In a small bowl, whisk egg whites, egg, pumpkin, brown sugar, and oil.

Add wet ingredients to dry ingredients, mixing until just combined. Fold in raisins.
Transfer batter to prepared pan. Bake at 350EF for about 60 minutes, or until a cake tester inserted into the center of the loaf comes out clean. Cool on a rack.

Serve warm or cold.

PUMPKIN SOUP   *Serves 4*

1 pumpkin, small

2 tablespoons butter

1 teaspoon sugar, granulated

1 teaspoon salt

1/4 teaspoon white pepper, ground fresh

3 cups milk, hot

As needed croutons

Cut pumpkin into wedges. Remove seeds and outer skin. Chop into small pieces.

In boiling, salted water, cook pumpkin until tender when tested with a fork. Drain and work through a sieve.

In a large saucepan, combine 2 cups pumpkin puree, butter, sugar, salt, and pepper. Cook over low heat about 10 minutes.

Stir in hot milk, a little at a time. Simmer gently for several minutes. Serve with croutons. Delicious!

Meat

Meat consisted of wild game, pork from hogs on the farm, a little beef, and sometimes chickens. Wild game - venison, rabbit, squirrel, duck, or turtle - was the major source of meat. Rarely was meat purchased before 1900. Meat was eaten fresh, dried, or smoked. Many homes in the pines had smoke-houses a few of which remain today.

Deer hunting was a community event. Hunters gathered in clubs which provided a source of cameraderie in addition to facilitating group hunting. The catch was shared by all.

ROAST VENISON

6-8 pounds venison rack
As needed butter or salt pork

Heat oven to 325°F.

Place meat in a roasting pan; allow it to reach room temperature.

Generously rub with butter, or cover with a piece of salt pork secured with string. If you use butter, baste occasionally during roasting period.

Roast the venison at 325°F for 18 minutes per pound. Do not overcook. Venison should be served rare, not well done.

Let roast stand on a warm platter before carving to allow

the juices to settle. Season to taste with salt and pepper.

Serve with potatoes, squash, or wild rice for a traditional hunters' meal.

VENISON MEAT LOAF   *Serves 6 to 8*

2 white bread slices, crusts removed
1 cup beef stock (or canned beef bouillon)
2 pounds venison, ground
1/4 pound salt pork, ground (optional)
1 onion, small, minced
1 garlic clove, minced
1/4 teaspoon black pepper, ground fresh
1/2 teaspoon salt
1 tablespoon parsley, minced
1 teaspoon mustard, prepared
2 tablespoons catsup
1 teaspoon Worcestershire sauce
3 or 4 bacon slices or salt pork

Heat oven to 350°F.

In a large bowl, soak bread in 2 cup beef stock. Add all remaining ingredients except bacon (or salt pork). Mix thoroughly.

To a shallow baking pan, transfer mixture and shape into a loaf. Place bacon (or salt pork slices) on top of loaf.

Bake at 350°F for approximately 1-1/2 hours, basting occasionally with pan juices. Remove to a warm serving platter. After removing meat loaf, add remaining beef stock to pan juices. Stir the added stock thoroughly over moderate heat, then simmer for about 10 minutes, strain, and pour over meat loaf.

VENISON POT ROAST *Serves 6 to 8*

Marinade

3 cups Burgundy or claret wine

1/2 cup vegetable oil

1/2 teaspoon black pepper, ground fresh

1 teaspoon salt

1 bay leaf (optional)

2 garlic cloves, minced

1 onion, small, chopped

2 teaspoons herbs (parsley, basil, tarragon, chives)

1 cup celery, diced

1 cup carrots, diced

Marinade

In a large pot, combine all ingredients; mix well.

Roast

1 4-5 pound venison roast

2 tablespoons butter

2 tablespoons vegetable oil

1/2 teaspoon salt

1/4 teaspoon black pepper, ground fresh
1-1/2 cups beef stock
2 onions, medium, chopped coarse
2 garlic cloves, chopped fine
2 teaspoons flour, all purpose

To marinade, add venison; turn meat until it is covered well with marinade. Cover and let stand for 6 hours at room temperature or 12 to 24 hours in refrigerator.
Remove roast, drain and dry. Reserve marinade.

In a heavy pot over moderate heat, melt butter with oil. Brown venison on all sides; remove from pan and sprinkle with salt and pepper.

To pot, add onions, cook slowly until transparent. Add garlic; cook 1 to 2 minutes.

Add flour to pan, blending thoroughly with fat, onions, and garlic. Add beef stock and 1/2 cup of reserved marinade; allow to simmer.

Place meat in pot, cover tightly. Over low heat cook until meat is tender. Time depends on the meat. Add more beef stock if needed. Turn meat at least once during cooking.

Remove meat from pot to heated platter. To liquids, add salt and pepper as needed. Strain into heated sauce boat.

Slice meat and pour a little sauce over each serving.

HUNTERS STYLE VENISON   *Serves 6*

3 pounds venison steak, cut into serving size pieces

2 teaspoon salt

5-6 peppercorns, cracked

1 carrot, sliced

1 onion, sliced

1 tablespoon parsley, chopped

1/2 teaspoon thyme, dried

1 bay leaf

1/2 cup red wine, dry

1/2 cup red wine vinegar

1/2 cup vegetable oil

as needed sour cream (optional)

In a large glass or ceramic bowl, combine salt, pepper, carrot, onion, parsley, thyme, wine, vinegar and 5 tablespoons oil; mix well. Add venison, and marinate in refrigerator for 2 hours, turning occasionally.

Remove meat from marinade. Pat dry with paper towels.

In a large frying pan, heat 3 tablespoons oil. Add meat and cook until all sides are nicely browned.

Add 1/2 cup marinade; cook, uncovered, over low heat until meat is tender. Add additional marinade if needed.

Remove meat from pan, arrange on a platter, and pour sauce from pan over meat.

If desired, add a few tablespoons of sour cream to sauce in the pan after meat has been removed.

PORK CHOPS AND SAUERKRAUT   *Serves 4*

4 pork chops, 1-inch thick

4-6 cups sauerkraut, drained, washed

1 onion, medium, chopped

1 cup apple juice

4 potatoes, white, medium, peeled, quartered

To taste salt and pepper

Heat oven to 350°F.

In a frying pan in a small amount of vegetable oil, brown chops; set aside.

Pour apple juice into pan and loosen brown bits.

In a 2-quart casserole, put kraut, onion, salt, and pepper. Put chops on top. Cover with apple juice. Tuck potatoes around the sides. Cover casserole with foil. Bake for 2 hours. Baste occasionally with liquid.

Serve piping hot!

ROAST WILD DUCK   *Serves 4*

2 2-1/2 pounds wild ducks, ready to cook
2 tablespoons butter, melted
1 teaspoon salt
1/2 cup celery leaves
2 apples, small, whole
2 onions, small, peeled
2 lemon slices
2 garlic cloves, optional
1/4 teaspoon black pepper, ground fresh
6 salt pork slices, thin
As needed Madeira Sauce

Heat oven to 350°F.

Soak ducks in salted water for about 1 hour. Drain and dry.

Rub cavities with melted butter, then salt. Inside the birds, place celery leaves, apples, onions, lemon slices, and garlic cloves. Sprinkle birds with salt and pepper.

Truss the birds. In an uncovered roasting pan, arrange birds, place salt pork slices over the breasts.

Bake at 350°F for 15 to 20 minutes per pound, basting frequently with pan juices.

Transfer birds to a heated serving platter, discarding trussing string and salt pork. Strain or pour off fat in roasting pan. Set aside.

Serve (1/2 duck per person) with Madeira Sauce.

Madeira Sauce   *Serves 4 to 6*

2 cups chicken stock (or canned chicken broth)

1 cup Madeira (or port) wine

2 duck livers, chopped coarse

to taste salt and pepper, ground fresh

1 tablespoon cornstarch (or arrowroot)

2 tablespoons water

To the roasting pan, add stock; over moderate heat, slowly scraping up all coagulated juices until dissolved.
Add Madeira (or Port) wine and cook until liquids are reduced to about 1-1/2 cups.

Add chopped livers; simmer over reduced heat another 5 minutes. Season to taste with salt and pepper.

In a small bowl, make a smooth paste with cornstarch and water; stir into sauce a little at a time until the desired consistency is obtained. The sauce should coat the spoon lightly. Serve sauce with duck.

CRANBERRY CHICKEN   *Serves 6*

3 chicken breasts, large, split in half, boned, skinned

1 cup flour, all purpose

To taste: salt, pepper, cayenne pepper

For frying: peanut oil

2 cups cranberry sauce, whole berry (homemade is best)

1/4 cup onion, chopped

3/4 cup orange juice

1/4 teaspoon cinnamon, ground

1/4 teaspoon ginger, ground

Heat oven to 350°F.
Wash and dry (with paper towels), the chicken breasts; set aside.

In a shallow dish, combine flour, salt, and pepper. Dredge each piece of chicken in flour mixture. Set aside.

In a large frying pan, heat peanut oil to point that a drop of water sizzles when added.

Fry chicken until just brown. Set aside in a glass baking dish.

In a stainless steel saucepan, combine other ingredients and bring to a boil. Pour over chicken.

Bake at 350°F for 35 to 40 minutes, until chicken is tender. Serve with sauce.

CHICKEN POT PIE   Serves 6

1 4-pound chicken
1 celery stalk, cut in chunks
1 carrot, cut in chunks
1 onion, stuck with 2 cloves
1 tablespoon salt
2 cups flour, all purpose
1/2 teaspoon salt
2 eggs
2-3 tablespoons water
4 potatoes, medium, peeled, sliced
6 parsley sprigs, minced

Cut chicken in serving size pieces. Place in a large kettle with celery, carrot, onion, salt, and cold water to cover.

Bring to a boil, cover; reduce heat, cook for about 40 minutes, or until chicken is tender when tested with a fork. Remove vegetables and discard. Remove chicken, cool; discard bones and skin; set aside. Reserve broth.

To make pot pie dough, into a medium bowl sift flour and salt. Dig a hole in the center, drop in egg, and blend to make a soft dough. Add 2-3 tablespoons of water as needed.

On a lightly floured board, roll dough as thin as possible. Cut into 1-inch squares; set aside.
Bring chicken broth to a boil. Drop potato slices and pas-

try slices into boiling broth, cover, and cook over moderate heat for 20 minutes. Add chicken pieces. To serve, ladle into warm soup plates; garnish with parsley.

CHICKEN FRICASSEE   *Serves 4*

1 4-5 pound chicken
1 cup water
1-1/2 teaspoons salt
dash pepper, ground fresh
1/4 cup butter
1/2 pound mushrooms, sliced (fresh or canned)
1 cup cream, half-and-half
1/2 teaspoon mace, ground
garnish parsley sprigs, chopped fine

Cut chicken into serving size pieces. Place in a heavy saucepan with tightly fitting lid. Add water, salt, and pepper. Over medium heat, bring to a boil; lower heat, cover tightly, and cook for about 1-1/2 hours, or until chicken is tender; set aside.

In a heavy saucepan, melt butter; add mushrooms and saute for about 5 minutes.

Add to chicken; add cream and mace. Cook over low heat for an additional 10 to 15 minutes.

To serve, arrange chicken pieces on a hot platter and spoon sauce over the top. Garnish with parsley.

BEEF STEW   *Serves 4*

2 tablespoons butter

1 onion, medium, chopped

2 pounds beef, cubed

2 tablespoon flour, all purpose

1 cup beef broth

3/4 teaspoon salt

1/4 teaspoon pepper, ground fresh

1/2 teaspoon savory, minced

1 teaspoon Worcestershire Sauce

1 teaspoon mustard, prepared

1/2 lemon, juice of

Garnish parsley sprigs, chopped

In a saucepan, melt butter; add onion and cook until wilted.

In a bowl, dust beef cubes with flour; add to onion and saute until brown on all sides.

Stir in broth, salt, pepper, and savory. Cover and cook over low heat for about 1-1/2 hours, or until beef is very tender. Stir in remaining ingredients. Delicious served with boiled potatoes.

FRIZZLED BEEF   *Serves 4*

2 tablespoons butter

1/4 pound beef, dried, shredded

3 tablespoons flour, all purpose

2 cups milk

Dash pepper, ground fresh

In a saucepan over low heat, melt butter; add dried beef; cook until edges begin to crisp.

Sprinkle in flour and continue cooking for 3 to 4 minutes, stirring constantly.

Pour in milk and cook, stirring until mixture bubbles and thickens. Season with pepper.

Serve over toast, biscuits, or fried Corn Meal Mush.

FRICASSEE RABBIT   *Serves 2*

1 rabbit, skinned, cleaned, cut in serving size portions

As needed seasoned flour

1/4 pound salt pork

1/4 cup onions, chopped

1 cup mushrooms, sliced

1-1/2 cups stock

To taste lemon rind

10 peppercorns

2 celery ribs, chopped

Dredge rabbit in seasoned flour; set aside.

In a large frying pan, fry salt pork. Saute onions and mushrooms. Remove and set aside.

In fat, brown rabbit on all sides.

Reduce heat and add stock, lemon rind, peppercorns, and celery. Return onions and mushrooms to pan.

Cover and simmer at low temperature for 1 hour or more.

SQUIRREL AND DUMPLINGS   *Serves 2*

1 squirrel, cleaned, cut in serving size pieces

1/4 teaspoon pepper, ground fresh

1 tablespoon butter

1/2 cup milk

To taste salt

In a large pot in salted water, over low heat, parboil squirrel for 10 minutes.

Remove squirrel; discard water. Add clean water to cover squirrel and cook until squirrel is tender. Add milk, butter, and pepper.

Prepare dumpling dough and drop into boiling liquid. Tightly cover pot and cook for 10 minutes, until dumplings are done.

Dumpling Dough

2 cups flour, all purpose
3 teaspoons baking powder
1 teaspoon salt
6-7 tablespoons shortening
2/3 to 3/4 cup milk

In a large bowl, sift together four, baking powder, and salt.

Cut in shortening until mixture has the consistency of coarse corn meal. Add milk and stir lightly with a fork.

Add to squirrel broth by tablespoonful.

Seafoods

The close by sea provided a variety of seafood which could be eaten fresh, dried, or smoked . The warm months of the year provided the opportunity to fish and gather shellfish to enjoy immediately or preserved for winter use. From the times of the Indians, local residents enjoyed the fruits of the sea.

CLAM FRITTERS *Makes 30 to 36 fritters; serves 4*

2 cups clams, chopped

2 cups flour, all purpose

2 teaspoons baking powder

1/2 teaspoon salt

1/4 teaspoon black pepper, ground fresh

Pinch cayenne pepper

1/2 cup milk

2 egg yolks, beaten

2 egg whites, beaten

As needed vegetable oil

Garnish lemon wedges

Garnish parsley sprigs

In a large bowl, sift flour with baking powder, salt, pepper, and cayenne; set aside.

Drain clams; save liquid. Measure liquid from clams and

add enough milk to make 1 cup; combine with egg yolks; mix well. Add liquids to flour mixture, stirring until batter is smooth. Fold in chopped clams.

Stir in 1 or 2 tablespoons of beaten egg whites, then carefully fold in remainder until no white streaks remain.

In a large skillet over moderate heat, heat 1/2 cup of oil. Immediately drop heaping tablespoonfuls of fritter batter. Cook until golden, turn, and cook on the other side.

Serve at once garnished with lemon wedges and parsley sprigs.

DEVILED CLAMS   *Serves 6*

12 clams, hard, medium

8-10 crackers (saltines)

1 onion, medium, peeled

1 tablespoon butter

2-4 bacon slices, chopped

Garnish parsley sprigs

Open clams, reserving liquid. Save shells for filling. Wash shells; set aside

Rinse clams in clam liquor. Set liquor aside until sediment settles. Strain through cheesecloth; save liquor.

Using the coarse blade of a food grinder, separately grind clams, crackers, and then onion; set aside.

In a frying pan in butter, saute onion until transparent; add clams and crackers. Mix in a little clam liquor for flavor. The crackers will thicken the mixture as it sets.

Fill clam shells with mixture, top with chopped bacon and parsley.

Place under broiler until hot and lightly browned. Serve while very hot.

This dish can be made ahead and frozen but it is best made fresh.

CLAM PIE   *Serves 6*
(A special recipe from Ada Applegate Brown, a Chatsworth resident.)

1 quart chowder clams, shucked, ground
6 bacon strips, fried crisp
3-4 potatoes, large, sliced
2 onions, large, sliced
1 cup celery, diced
2 carrots, shredded (optional)
4 eggs, hard cooked
1/2 cup parsley, fresh, chopped
1 crust, double for deep dish pie

Heat oven to 450°F.

In bacon fat, cook onions and celery until onions are opaque. Add juice drained from clams, potatoes, carrots, and parsley.

Cook until potatoes are tender. Add clams.

Fit bottom crust in deep dish pie plate. Fill with clam mixture. Top with quartered eggs and top crust. Flute edges of crust to seal and make a high rim.

Bake at 450°F for 15 minutes. Lower temperature to 375°F and bake an additional 45 minutes, or until crust is nicely browned. Let pie sit for 10 to 15 minutes before cutting.

CLAM (QUAHOG) CHOWDER   *Serves 8-10*

1 quart clams, shucked, drained

1/4 pound salt pork, diced 1/2-inch

2 onions, medium, diced

4 potatoes, medium, peeled, diced

4 cups milk (or half milk and half evaporated milk)

To taste salt

1/4 teaspoon black pepper, ground fresh

Remove clams from liquor; strain liquor through cheese-cloth; set aside. Reserve liquor.

Chop clams coarse.

In a heavy pot over moderate heat, cook salt pork until crisp and golden. Remove, dice; drain on paper towels; set aside.

To fat in pot, add onions. Cook until tender and transparent.

Add potatoes, then clam liquor, and water to rise about 1-inch above the potatoes. Simmer, covered, until potatoes are tender. Add clams; simmer an additional 5 minutes.

In a saucepan, heat the milk with butter; do not allow to boil. Add to chowder pot. Season with salt and pepper to taste.

Remove pot from heat and allow chowder to >age= for an hour or two in the refrigerator.

Over low heat, reheat, uncovered, until chowder steams. Do NOT allow to boil. Remove from heat and serve with a dollop of butter. Chowder is always better the second day!

SCALLOPED OYSTERS   *Serves 4*

1 pint oysters, shucked, drained

1/4 cup oyster liquor

2 tablespoonscream, light

1/2 cup bread crumbs, day old

1 cup cracker crumbs

1/2 cup butter, melted

To taste salt

To taste pepper, ground fresh

Garnish paprika

Heat oven to 425°F. Butter a 1-quart casserole. Sprinkle with a thin layer of bread crumbs on bottom; set aside.

In a small bowl, combine oyster liquor and cream; set aside.

In another small bowl, combine crumbs with melted butter; set aside.

In the casserole, cover bottom with half the oysters and half the liquor-cream mix. Season with salt and pepper.

Add second layer of crumbs, then oysters; add remaining liquor-cream mix. Sprinkle with remaining crumbs and paprika.

Bake in 425°F for 30 minutes. Serve!

OYSTER PIE *Serves 4*

1 pint oysters, shucked
3 tablespoons butter
1/4 pound mushrooms, fresh, sliced
3 tablespoons flour, all purpose
1 cup cream, half-and-half
1/2 teaspoon salt
1/4 teaspoon pepper, white
dash Worcestershire sauce
1 teaspoon lemon juice
Garnish cayenne pepper
1 pastry crust

Heat oven to 425°F.

Drain oysters, reserving liquor.

In a heavy skillet over moderate heat, melt 2 tablespoons butter. Add mushrooms and cook until lightly browned, about 5 minutes. Remove mushrooms and set aside.

To skillet add remaining butter; when melted add flour and stir until well blended. Cook for 1 minute.

Strain oyster liquor; combine with enough cream to make 1-1/2 cups. Add to skillet, reduce heat, and cook, stirring constantly, until mixture thickens. Remove from heat.

Add oysters, salt, pepper, mushrooms, Worcestershire sauce, lemon juice, and cayenne pepper.

Into a round, shallow 8-inch casserole, pour mixture. Cover with pastry crust, rolled about 1/4 inch thick. Slash crust.

Bake at 425°F for 10 to 15 minutes, or until crust begins to brown. Reduce heat to 375EF and bake an additional 15 to 20 minutes. Serve piping hot.

CODFISH CHOWDER   *Serves 6 to 8*

1 4-pound cod, fresh, cleaned
1 salt pork cube, 2x2-inches, diced
1 onion, medium, sliced
6 cups potatoes, peeled, sliced thin
4 cups milk
1 tablespoon salt
1/4 teaspoon pepper, ground fresh
3 tablespoons butter
8 common crackers, split in half

Skin and fillet fish; save fish head, tail, backbone, and other trimmings. Cut cod fillet in 2-inch pieces; set aside.

In a large saucepan with 2 cups water, add fish head, tails, trimmings. Heat to boiling, reduce heat, and cook slowly for about 20 minutes; set aside.

In a stock pot over low heat, cook salt pork until crisp. Add onion and cook until limp.

In a large saucepan in salted water, cook potatoes about 5 minutes; drain.

Add potatoes and 2 cups of boiling water to salt pork mixture. Cook 5 minutes. Add liquor from fish bones. Add cod. Cover and simmer for 10 minutes.

In a saucepan, scald milk. Add to fish mixture. Season with

salt and pepper, to taste. Add butter and crackers. Heat until piping hot. Chowder is always better the second day than the first!

BAKED BLUEFISH   *Serves 6*

1 4 to 4-1/2 pound bluefish, cleaned

As needed vegetable oil

to taste   Salt and pepper, ground fresh

1 tablespoon onion, minced

3/4 cup tomato juice

3/4 cup bread crumbs, fresh

2 tablespoons butter, melted

Heat oven to 350°F.

In a shallow, well-oiled baking pan, lay fish. Rub fish skin with oil; season with salt and pepper.

Scatter onion over fish. Add tomato juice to pan.

Bake in 350°F for 30 minutes, basting occasionally with tomato juice.

In a small bowl, combine butter and bread crumbs; mix well. Sprinkle over fish.

Broil fish, 4 inches from heat, until browned. Fish should flake easily when tested with a fork. Serve!

CODFISH CAKES   *Serves 4*

1/2 pound codfish, salt dried

1/2 onion, medium diced fine

1-1/2 cups potatoes, cooked, mashed

To taste pepper, ground fresh

As needed: flour, all purpose

For frying: peanut oil

In a large saucepan, cover cod with water and bring to a boil. Pour off water and repeat three times to freshen cod.

Drain; when cool, pick out bones carefully.

In a large bowl, combine fish, onion, and mashed potatoes. Form mixture into four 5-inch patties; dip in flour. Set aside.

In a large frying pan, heat oil; fry patties until golden brown on both sides. The patties also can be baked in 350°F for 10 minutes. Serve piping hot!

CLAM POT PIE   *Serves 6*

Betty Lamson West, a New Gretna native, allowed her family recipe for Clam Pot Pie to be published in the Bass River Gazette in 2002. Recognized as a great cook, her Clam Pot Pie was a favorite of her family, relatives, and friends. We share it with you. (Bass River Gazette 13, Jul-Dec, 2002)

40 clams, medium, opened, ready to chop

1/4 pound salt pork, cut in small pieces
6 potatoes, medium, peeled, sliced
2 cups onions, chopped in small pieces
To taste salt and pepper

Drain juice from clams; reserve 1 cup. Set aside clams.
In a large pot (6-quart Dutch oven), over medium heat, cook
salt pork until tender and brown; stir frequently.

Chop clams into small pieces. Set aside.

To salt pork, add potatoes and onions. Cover ingredients
with 2 cups water and 1 cup clam juice. Simmer 10 minutes.

Add chopped clams. Drop Biscuit Dough by tablespoonfuls
into broth. Keep lid tightly on pot (Dutch oven) as biscuit
dough simmers. Allow 20 to 30 minutes for the dough to
cook.

Serve piping hot.

Biscuit Dough

2 cups flour, all purpose
3 teaspoons baking powder
1 teaspoon salt
6-7 tablespoons shortening
2/3-3/4 cup milk

In a large bowl, sift together flour, baking powder, and salt.

Cut in shortening until mixture has the consistency of coarse corn meal. Add milk and stir lightly with a fork.

Add to clam broth by tablespoonfuls.

The snapper, Chelydra serpentina, is a mean-tempered, aggressive, ugly creature, a turtle. How it first made its way into the cook pot is unknown. Today and for years, it has been an important and prized item in pineland dwellers' diet.

After a snapper is captured (that's another story), it must be "purged." This is done by placing it into a barrel of water. The snapper is then killed by beheading. The body is hung to bleed for a while, then boiled. The skin is removed, the shell cut away, and the snapper cut into six pieces - the legs, tail, and neck. The meat is placed in a pot and boiled until tender, then removed.

The vegetables, usually potatoes, carrots, and onions along with spices of the cook's choice, are simmered in the broth. Once the vegetables are done, the meat is returned to the pot and it is ready to be served.

AUNT PEG'S SNAPPER SOUP
(From the Rev. Wayne Reynolds, Tuckerton, NJ)

Flour
Bacon drippings
Snapper meat, shredded
String beans
Cabbage, shredded
Potatoes, peeled, diced
Celery, diced
Onions, sliced
Carrots, sliced
Peas
Butter
Eggs, hard cooked, ground
Water
White wine

In a large pot, combine flour and bacon drippings to make a roux. Cook until golden brown.

Stir in cabbage, potatoes, celery, onions, and carrots. When the vegetables are coated with roux, add water and white wine, enough to almost fill the pot.

Add snapper meat, string beans and peas; bring to a gentle boil. Reduce heat and add butter, almost 1 pound for each 3 pounds of snapper meat.

Add hard cooked eggs. Cook for 3 to 4 hours.

ALICE WEBER'S WHITEHOUSE SNAPPER SOUP
Serves 6 to 8 (From Bass River Gazette 7, May-Sep, 2000)

Boil snapping turtle with 3 ounces Seafood Base or 1 table-spoon salt until tender. Remove turtle from stock, strain and reserve. When cooled, remove meat from bone, discard bones.

1-1/2 pounds turtle meat
2-3/4 teaspoons salt
3/4 teaspoon cayenne
6 cups water
1 stick butter
1/2 cup flour, all purpose
1-1/2 cups onions, chopped
2 tablespoons shallots, minced
14 cup bell peppers, chopped
1/4 cup celery, chopped
3 bay leaves
1/2 teaspoon thyme leaves, dried
2 tablespoons garlic, minced
1 cup tomatoes, chopped
1/2 cup Worcestershire sauce
3 tablespoons lemon juice, fresh
1/2 cup Sherry, dry
1/4 cup parsley, chopped
1/2 cup green onions, chopped
4 eggs, cooked hard, shelled, chopped fine
2 tablespoons green onions, chopped
2 tablespoons eggs, hard cooked, shelled, chopped

In a large pot, combine turtle meat, 1 teaspoon salt, 1/4 teaspoon cayenne and the water. Bring to a boil. Skim off any foam that rises to the top. Reduce heat to medium and simmer for 20 minutes. With a slotted spoon transfer the meat to a platter.

Cut meat into 1/2 inch dice and reserve the liquid.

In another large sauce pan, combine the butter and flour over medium heat, stirring constantly, for 6 to 8 minutes, to make a dark roux.

Add the onions, shallots, bell peppers, and celery. Stir occasionally and cook for 2 to 3 minutes until the vegetables are slightly tender.

Add the bay leaves, thyme, and garlic; cook for 2 minutes.

Add the tomatoes and turtle meat. Cook for 5 to 6 minutes, stirring occasionally.

Add the Worcestershire sauce, the remaining salt and cayenne, the turtle stock (about 6 cups), lemon juice, and sherry.

Bring to a boil, reduce heat to medium and simmer for 10 minutes.

Add the parsley, green onions, and eggs; simmer for 45 minutes.

Garnish with green onions and chopped eggs. Serve!

REFERENCES

American Heritage Cookbook, Vol. I & II., American Heritage Publishing Co., Inc. (1964)

Bass River Gazette. Various issues.

Brown, Robert and Marion. Personal communication

Cohen, David Steven. The Folklore and Folklife of New Jersey. Rutgers University Press, New Brunswick, NJ (1991).

Estlow, Ethel. Personal communication

Fischer, David Hackett. Albion=s Seed: Four British Folkways in America. Oxford Univrsity Press, Oxford (1989)

Moonsommy, Rita Zorn, Cohen, David Steven, and Williams, Lorraine, Editors. Pinelands Folklife. Rutgers University, New Brunswick, NJ (1987)

Simmons, Amelia, American Cookery (1796)

APPLES

BLACKBERRIES

BLUEBERRIES

CORN

CRANBERRIES

DESSERTS

TREATS

VEGETABLES

About the Author

R. Marilyn Schmidt is the author of almost 70 books. She has spent many years researching the New Jersey Pine Barrens. She painstakingly took on the task of clearing the title for Buzby's Chatsworth General Store, located in Chatsworth, New Jersey (the heart of the Pine Barrens) and then renovating the store back to its original condition as much as possible. The store has once again become a meeting place for those interested in the culture and history of the Pine Barrens.

Area residents consider Marilyn to be "an adopted Piney," a title bestowed on precious few folks. It is the title she wears most proudly, although in her lifetime she has claimed many other hats: in addition to being a certified tax assessor and author, she has worked as a biochemist and a pharmacologist. She has a real estate license and has done pottery and painting in her "spare time." It is the latter she hopes to return to when she retires.

Other Fine Titles by R. Marilyn Schmidt:

Cookbooklets for every type of fish, sure to answer the question: What's for dinner tonight? If you love fish but are tired of the same way of cooking it, these cookbooklets will delight your palate.

Blackfish / Tautog	Scallops
Blue Crab	Sea Bass
Caviar	Seafood Chowders, Soups & Bisques
Cod & Pollock	Seafood Salads
Eastern Oysters	Seafood Stir Fry
Flounder & Other Flat Fish	Shad Shad Roe
Hard Shell Clams	Shrimp
Lobsters, North American	Soft Shell Clams
Mackerel, Atlantic/Spanish	Squid
Mahi-Mahi	Sturgeon
Mako Shark	Tilefish
Monkfish	Tilipia / St. Peter's Fish
Mussels	Tuna
Orange Roughy	Weakfish / SeaTrout
Salmon	

A Sampler of Canned Seafood

Here's your answer to serving unexpected or expected guests a gourmet meal! From your pantry you can serve appetizers, salads and entrees from a wide variety of canned seafood: anchovies, clams, conch, crab, herring, lobster, mackerel, oysters, salmon, sardines, shrimp, and of course, tuna. Learn the best ways for handling canned seafood.

Bargain Seafoods

Bargain seafood, sometimes called "trash fish" are those in abundance and sometimes discarded by fisherman. These seafood are underappreciated. Wonderful flavors and economical prices await you. Try Atlantic Mackerel, Atlantic Pollock, Butterfish, Croaker, Cusk, Dogfish, Eel, Ling or Red Hake, Mussels, Sea Robins, Sharks, Skates and Rays, Smelts, and Whiting or Silver Lake. All are delicious!

Chutney Complete

Chutneys, easy to make, versatile, and distinctive, preserve fresh vegetables and fruit for year round use. Making chutney is almost foolproof, not like jellies and jams. Chutneys make great gifts. Serve with meats, cheeses, or just on crackers.

Cooking the Shore Catch

New Jersey's seafood at its finest! Traditional recipes for both finfish and shellfish from Sandy Hook to Cape May enable you to cook everyone's favorites. Recipes from fisherman and their wives, some long gone and those here today. A must for those who "go down the shore." Recipes are for seafood caught commonly in New Jersey's waters.

Flavored Vinegars

Flavored vinegars are an "in" product. Easy to make, great to use. Here are directions for making over 32 different vinegars and vinaigrettes. Give a unique gift of your own special vinegar. Use the extra herbs from your garden.

Herb Sauces, Salsas, and Such

Tired of paying high prices for seasonings and sauces? Make your own! Here are recipes for 75 herb-flavored condiments. Perfect for gifts, delicious to taste, and inexpensive to make. Use your own herb crop for a top quality product.

How to Write a Family Cookbook

Ever wonder how your grandmother made that fantastic stew? Do your kids ask for favorite family recipes? Why not preserve these favorites for future generations? This booklet gives briefly the "how to" of writing and publishing your family cookbook. This is a perfect gift for family and friends.

Mustard Magic

Grow your own mustard plants and make mustards from your crop, or from purchased dry mustard and seeds. Recipes are included for making 32 mustards and 15 mustard sauces and dressings. Try making your own special mustard. Great gifts!

Seafood Secrets:
A Nutritional Guide to Seafood

We live in a health conscious era. Daily we are bombarded by articles on weight control, heart disease, diet and drugs. Diet is important – essentially, you are what you eat! Recently, seafood has been emphasized as "heart food." Why? Research data confirms that increased fish consumption leads to reduced risk of heart disease. There are often questions concerning whether a particular fish or shellfish is allowed on our specific diet. Often questions arise such as "Can I eat scallops when I have to watch my cholesterol level?" or "Is saltwater fish too high in salt for my low salt diet?" This book supplies you with the answers to these questions and the basic information needed to guide you in the selection of seafood for your special dietary needs. Cooking and health hints will guide you in how to reduce the calories in your favorite recipes.

Seafood Smoking, Grilling, Barbecuing

Use your grill to cook an entire meal! Here are recipes for finfish and shellfish plus recipes for sauces and directions for grilling fruits and vegetables, too. Just think, no pans to wash. Your entire dinner is on the grill.

All titles can be purchased on line at: www.pinebarrenspress.com. Most of the books can also be purchased at Amazon, both in paperback and for Kindle.

Wholesale prices are also available for bulk quantities. Please call 609.758.1304 or send an email to info@kfrcommunications.com for more information.

Made in the USA
Charleston, SC
06 March 2012